• **Praise for *Called Back*** •

"The momentum of *Called Back* . . . derives from [Mary Cappello's] extraordinarily capacious mind: her intelligence, wit, and emotional candor; the clarity and alertness of her train of thought; the restlessness of her style. . . . Cappello makes stunning connections between literature, art, her life, medicine, cancer. A brilliant book."

—David Shields, author of
The Thing About Life is One Day You'll Be Dead,
and *Reality Hunger*

"I loved being offered the companionship of Cappello's *feeling* mind. . . . I loved her insistence on taking everything in, not rushing to be 'healed' before experience registers. I loved the precision and passion with which this book about facing mortality attends to the particulars of being alive—both in the body and in language."

—Jan Clausen, author of *If You Like Difficulty*,
and *From a Glass House*, and *Apples and Oranges:
My Journey through Sexual Identity*

• **Praise for *Night Bloom*** •

" . . . her writing shines, and, like the flowers she cherishes, offers fleeting glimpses of beauty."

—*The New York Times Book Review*

"The literature of immigration has produced such notable works as the novels *Giants in the Earth* and *Call It Sleep*. . . . Cappello's book can take an honorable place among them." —*Booklist*

"When I first encountered Mary Cappello's work, I was knocked out by her original voice, the juxtaposition of its fierceness and elegance, its brutality and gentleness, its sensuousness and intelligence. She's a writer whose debut memoir you can't miss; she's a writer you'll tell all your friends about, as I did."

—Louise DeSalvo, author of *Vertigo*

W9-AGV-718

• Praise for *Awkward: A Detour* •

"At once comforting and startling, *Awkward: A Detour* is a new kind of memoir, each sentence more of a discovery than a reporting back. The fluent subtlety of Cappello's adventurous meditation—her talent for atmosphere and for letting certain words get the better of her—makes memory seem like something worth re-making, and not the casual currency it has become. It is a remarkable achievement."

—Adam Phillips, author of
Terrors and Experts, On Kissing, Tickling and Being Bored: Psychoanalytic Essays on the Unexamined Life,
and *Going Sane: Maps of Happiness*

"A wonderful, multi-layered piece of writing, with all the insight of great cultural criticism and all the emotional pull of memoir. A fascinating book."

—Sarah Waters, author of
Tipping the Velvet and *The Night Watch*

"'I would seek out awkwardness over and against revelation,' Mary Cappello writes, and her inventive, associative taxonomy of discomfort does exactly that, investigating the terms we use for those moments when we're 'uncoordinated,' 'clueless,' 'ass-backwards'— moments which turn out, in her patient and eager excavations, to be revelatory indeed."

—Mark Doty, author of
Fire to Fire: New and Selected Poems

Called Back

MY REPLY TO CANCER

•

MY RETURN TO LIFE

Called Back

MARY CAPPELLO

ALYSON books

Published by Alyson Books
245 West 17th Street, Suite 1200, New York, NY 10011
www.alyson.com

ALYSONbooks

A version of the first chapter appeared in the Summer 2009 issue of *The Georgia Review* under the title "Getting the News: A Signer Among Signs." The Coda appeared in the Fall 2009 issue of *The Seattle Review*.

Library of Congress Cataloging-in-Publication data is on file.

ISBN-10: 1-59350-150-1
ISBN-13: 978-1-59350-150-1

10 9 8 7 6 5 4 3 2 1

Cover design by Lorie Pagnozzi
Book interior by Elyse Strongin, Neuwirth & Associates, Inc.

Printed in the United States of America
Distributed by Consortium Book Sales and Distribution
Distribution in the United Kingdom by Turnaround Publisher Services Ltd

For Deidre Pope, Alice Lee, Carol Sepe,
Steve Jacobson, Jon Hendrickson

their expertise and

loving care,

their laying on

of hands and words

CONTENTS

" . . . the number of events it takes to create the probable sequence
Necessary to cause a change in any person's state
Is far larger than one might think
Therefore any account of it
Must be very long
And during all that time
Reality moves around
Changing orientation . . . "

—LYN HEJINIAN
A Border Comedy

"I am talking here about the need for every woman to live a
considered life."

—AUDRE LORDE
The Cancer Journals

Called Back

· 1 ·

Diagnosis:

news

God hasn't forgotten me.
Look—he sent an illness!

—Russian Proverb

at first there were only looks and very few words. I didn't even have a name, so I asked her her name, assuming that if I called her by her name, I might begin to have one.

"She" was the ultrasound technician who was examining an image of the inner contours of my breast on a screen. Prior to my meeting her, there had been a mammography technician who called me back into her room in the hope of gaining a better purchase on the mystery, on getting the machine to hone in, to bore down into, to see. Behind the scenes, I also knew there was a doctor. Invisible as Oz's wizard, she was planted somewhere, in an inner sanctum, *reading*. She was neither chewing gum nor drinking coffee in my mind's eye; she wasn't leafing through the empty paragraphs of a waiting room's magazines; she was *reading*, undistracted I hoped, by her love life, the pain in her left foot that was requiring an undue emphasis on the right, the impending visit from her estranged daughter, the whiff of a near nightmare she'd had the night before, the matter of her refrigerator seeming to be on the fritz with the

3

dinner party upcoming, or the unsettling because no longer disturbing news of that morning's death toll from Iraq.

Mammograms, there's no question, are painfully unpleasant, but at least you *stand* for them. In the ultrasound room, you are supine—which, in medical situations, as far as I'm concerned, is never good. Rather than look at the screen, I watched the ultrasound technician watching. I tried to read her face. It was peering, and at a certain point it became more alert, the way a scuba diver's might when he's found the endangered anemone he was in search of. But this nearly jubilant alertness turned almost immediately into its opposite. The nameless woman's face turned, there is only one word for it, grave. She gave me her face, her sad face, and she said, "You stay right here while I show this to the doctor."

Now the doctor and the technician returned together, the wizard revealing herself to be simultaneously buxom and long-nosed, a kind of Wallace and Gromit figure with a British accent, not a mainland British accent but the tonally differentiated purl of someone reared at a colony. My guess: either South Africa or New Zealand. She neither asked me my name nor greeted me, but hurried. She bustled all aflutter toward the screen as she took the matter literally into her hands. She began to wield the ultrasound wand as if to suggest that if she did this herself, she'd see something different and better than the technician had. The doctor didn't quite know how to angle the instrument, so the technician helped her saying, "Do you see the shadow?" "And the peaks?" The words recommended to me a painting by Caspar David Friedrich.

Now the doctor looked at me as though I were an out of focus text and she was without her reading glasses. "Yes, you need to arrange to have a biopsy. This is concerning," she said. And I said, "But I'm leaving town tomorrow. I'm a writer, and I have a new book just out, and I'm giving a series of readings from it beginning in California." She looked at me sadly and said, "You'll have to figure something out." And then she left the room.

"What's your name?" I said to the ultrasound technician.

"Joan," she said, and I said, "Joan, my name is Mary. Can you tell me something about what you're seeing?" And she used the doctor's word, "Well, it's concerning," she said. "It's suspicious." The euphemisms were coming thick and fast, and then her face turned grave again, and I thought she was going to say, "It's your cat, your little cat with the graceful lilt and upturned tail, something fell on your cat and smothered her, and well, she's dead," but what she said was, moving her head to one side as though she knew I would want to punch it, "It's definitely not a cyst."

"So what does that mean?" I asked.

"It means it's a mass. It's concerning."

I'm not sure at what point I moved from lying down to sitting up, but I remember saying to Joan, as though I didn't have to think about it, the words came so naturally, I said, "I guess it's my turn." Joan gasped a little, my words annoyed her, and she addressed me as though I were saying something self-punishing or inappropriately not nice about myself. "Don't say that!" she said, still with the long face. So I explained myself because Joan clearly wasn't understanding me. I said, "I'm not saying I'm going to die, but every other woman I know has cancer, so I'm just saying I guess it's my turn. I mean why *shouldn't* I have it?" And hearing myself say this, I cried a little, but not for long because I knew I had to gather my real clothes from their locker and I didn't want to disturb the other women in the waiting room. I didn't want them to know what I was being told about myself, so I quickly wiped my tears.

Now Joan offered help. She told me they were going to call my gynecologist and that maybe the biopsy could be performed that afternoon. "So this is him, right, that's Dr. Timothy Speers?" she asked, looking at a chart, and I corrected her, "No, it's Dr. Beaumont, Rene Beaumont." She showed me the form with the wrong name on it, and I noticed that the name of the radiologist was wrong, too, because I'd just met the buxom woman with the long nose and I don't think her name was James L. Fraser, M.D. Maybe this world was like marriage: all of the female doctors had to take on the names of their male peers. It was clear to me I was entering a world in which names didn't matter, nor words, when both were everything to me.

⌐

I'm amazed by how my mind never slows down, how it gathers together in a flash multiple points of compatible referents as a means of making sense of things, or is that only something it's doing now, confronted as it appears to be by the c-word: not the dirty word for woman, nor the kiddy name for shit, but the rampant and yet still tabooed emblem for a disease entity that scrabbles sideways like its namesake among crustaceans and hosts patterns much less wondrous than fractals. I'm sure through the right set of eyes something marvelous must lurk inside a c- cell, not only something horrifying.

Joan had cut a path through my gynecologist's waiting room upstairs, and within an hour I was seeing her but with a different sense than I had ever felt before: suddenly I was in love with my gynecologist for the way she stood for someone I had known and in whose care I'd been—however routine that was and intermittent. She introduced me to a word other than "mass."

"So it's not a cyst," I said, and she said, "The thing about it is that it's *solid*. Ultrasound is very good at telling the difference. And it could be a kind of fibrous mass that women get, but the thing that is *concerning* is that its edges are ragged where the edges of most benign tumors are smooth." Prior to trusting me with such an important distinction, she had complimented me on finding the lump because she found it hard to feel as she examined me. She shared her sense of hopefulness that it was small.

"Would that this too, too solid flesh would melt, thaw, and resolve itself into a dew." Literary references immediately entered my mind. I felt like reciting Hamlet's words, but checked myself! Alice James' description of the lump in her breast also occurred to me, and almost as though her impeccably wise face were nearby, Susan Sontag whispered to me a line from *Illness as Metaphor* about illness depositing a person onto "an island of difference." (I heard this line even though nothing about a potential breast c-diagnosis made me feel "distinct." It's really utterly banal.)

Watch the mind so as not to spin off course try to interpret the situation it finds itself in with metaphors. Without metaphors, I'm hopelessly alone. *With* metaphors, I'm *like*, I'm kin. So I gave myself, not trying to, I gave myself two metaphors when I went back to get my clothes outside the room where I'd earlier chatted with the other women and even made them laugh as together, waiting, we blankly faced the obligatory TV screen whose loop of tales of necessary prophylaxis against all the illnesses in the world, and hopeful skits about autistic boys who do karate, and quizzes about which fruit juice was best for your kidneys, went around and around and around like an idiotic song on a player piano. Two metaphors tried to help me imagine what I had become, or at least what I *felt* like: the first was an image of a rotten apple discovered among the good apples. Maybe because our smocks were red. I'd been identified as rotten, or at least rotting, and picked out from among the barrel of women in the waiting room to be deposited somewhere else. Fast upon the rotten apple idea, I thought of someone else I felt like: the person taken out of line for execution. Somebody had to be picked, and this is what it felt like. This particular raft, however bereft, bobbed consolingly up to the surface out of the basement suite of a storehouse of movie images that I, like anyone else, have stowed in my tiny, struggling brain.

This is what it feels like to be the one arbitrarily pulled out of line. "Go with that!" I told myself. Hmmm. It's not the same as being chosen or not for a team in the lineup in gym class, but images of adolescent popularity or lack thereof hung nearby.

Other images I gave myself were more implicitly soothing. Lying on my side, readying myself for a biopsy—no one had ever described to me the parts of this procedure—I'd hoped to gaze at the ocean mural painted by a student from the Rhode Island School of Design onto one of the hospital's ceiling panels. But the gurney got pulled around, turning the image upside down. The steps of a core biopsy go like this, and, remember, you're awake: first a needle filled with local anesthetic is inserted into the affected breast. Then a small incision is made through which a doctor guides a tube, into which she inserts an instrument that she'll use to take samples of the tumor, the contours of which she simultaneously watches on an ultrasound screen. She needs to withdraw five samples minimum and the instrument makes a loud stapling sound with each extraction. Sometimes the samples "break up," and she has to take more.

I told myself I was of "strong peasant stock," and called up an image of my great-grandmother, all of whose six children but one died in childhood. At a certain point in the litany of child deaths, she made a pilgrimage to Rome where she climbed the Scala Sancta, penitently, on her knees. "This is nothing!" I told myself, and when the doctor and technician beheld my calm—"You didn't even flinch!" they said—I lied a little: I told them I had practiced Tai Chi.

They sent me home with a prescription: "Go out and buy six bags of frozen peas," Maya, the technician, said, "and keep them tucked inside a tight fitting bra for the next twenty-four hours. That's going to be the best thing you can do for yourself." Again, an image came: this time, in the form of a memory, of an afternoon of terrific heat in a town outside Milan. It never got so hot there; no one had air conditioners, and the two pugs of the woman I was staying with were nearly hyperventilating. So she applied a pack of frozen peas to the sides of their heaving jowls, but the method didn't work well because the dogs in each case bit through the bags and ate the peas.

Given a choice between descriptors for your tumor, which would you prefer? That the edges be "ragged," "pointed," "peaked," "star-like," "spiculated," or "finger-like"? Does a tumor's edge by any other name rage as fiercely? Each of these adjectives was delivered to me in a twenty-four hour period, and I was struck by their range. A finger has to be unfurled, a peak scaled, a star—well, a star is simply beyond reach, but I appreciated it for its fanciful dimensions. As though the sheriff's badge I wore as a kid embedded itself, as though the fairy who'd touched the tip of her wand to me while I was sleeping, meaning to bejewel me, had harmed me. In an ultrasound image, edges look like pieces of a moth's wing, the moth caught inside your chest, the tumor's changing form, its batting. "Ragged" suggests unkempt. "Star-like" invokes the heavens. "Fingers" emit a body within the body that can encroach, grab, and strangle. As such, finger-like is my least favorite descriptor.

Words *do* matter, and yet there's a way in which a tumor is like nothing but itself in that same way that each of us is told by someone in the earliest days of our lives, when everyone is saying, "You look like your mother!", "You look like your father!," one brave, wise soul looks you in the eye and says, "You look like nobody but yourself."

~~~

Words do matter. What if instead of saying, "I have breast cancer," I said I had EPM—Environmental Pollutant Marker or, if you prefer, Environmental Pollutant Mangler? Or PPP—Plastic Polymer Perverter? I'm not "suffering" from anything just yet: PPP in its earliest stages is symptomless. In fact, I've never felt better in my life. I've only been duped, despoiled by global capitalism and imperialism, in which case, I'm a benighted victim of GCI syndrome, just like you, and I was such a "productive citizen," too.

Names are key. The answering machine can be a devilish device once the news is out.

Message #1: "Hi you guys, it's Lori White. I just got the news of Jeannie's diagnosis from Laura in an e-mail, and I just want to give you such positive thoughts. Having beat this myself, there's so much to be hopeful about, Jeannie, and I really want to talk to you. I hope you'll call me tonight. . . . Tomorrow I'm participating in a triathalon. I'm in great shape, and I'm going to show the world I can run a triathalon with one breast! I hope you'll call me!"

Message #2: "Uh, Jeannie, Mary, I'm so sorry. I just re-read Laura's message and I see it's Mary who has cancer. Mary, I'm so sorry. To be honest, I was a little bit in shock when I read the news and I wasn't thinking clearly. So, *Mary*, I hope you'll give me a call because I really want to talk to you about this, ok?"

You can't blame people. Their being upset must be a sign that they love you, right? But you perhaps should be forewarned that their reading and listening faculties are likely to go awry at this time, so you'll have to keep them on track and stay clear for them.

Mary: "Hi Lewis, it's Mary. I know you got the message that it *is* cancer..."

Lewis: "Oh my God, Mare, I can't believe it, do you really have stage 5, cancer then?"

I had explained to this beloved friend, face to face in my garden, that the radiologist's *code* for my tumor was 5, or "highly suggestive of malignancy," but *stage* 5 cancer? I had to explain to him that if I had stage 5 cancer I'd be dead.

Language matters, and if you take a kabbalistic approach, you might fear people's misuse of words as predictive, prophetic. Jeannie's diagnosis! Stage 5 cancer! I'm not paranoid, but I have a sudden fervent need to stay away from these people or at least find ways to fend off their readerly ineptitude.

"Is there breast cancer in your family" somebody asks, hoping to take the genetic approach rather than the PPP approach.

There's not a single case of breast cancer in my entire extended family, I point out, only cancer of the blood, liver, lung, vocalcords, and brain.

Language matters: positive in cancerland means negative. Dear friends: please stop sending me positive thoughts. Besides which, as valences, positive and negative aren't all they're cracked up to be; besides which, positive and negative are joined at the hip in the name of the same.

Would that, would that, were it that, wish it so. A wall has gone up inside me and behind it I hear a hammering in spite of a splendid morning bike ride on the day I'm set to get "the news." But I haven't stopped noticing things. To notice is to know, to announce your own "new," singular or plural, to be perceiving. It's hard, though, to see beyond predetermined signs: the predictably claustrophobic edges of the waiting room's walls, jutting. An office plant. Am I the only one to see "nipple" in Nate Whipple Radiology, one of many pamphlets stacked in a row for my reading pleasure?

If it were up to me, the whole waiting room gestalt would be different. There should be velvet; light food and drink; the invitation to sing; rich colors, low lights, and crayons; the expectation of mutual massage.

When I set my table, I have my guests in mind. I choose my favorite glasses, my most beautiful plates. I set water and wine within reach, and fruit, as much for its color as for its texture and taste. And my living room—it has others in mind too: that's why the orchid plant that finally bloomed this year, and the books, face the chair I know a friend will sit in.

From waiting room to newsroom—I thought the surgeon whom my gynecologist had recommended would take us into a consulting room, but he chose the examining room to share the news. Which means he'll still be in charge, his subject to my object, my being subject to his. What can you notice in the worst five minutes worth of waiting in your life, waiting for "the news"?

I notice that the wallpaper is torn as though someone in desperation had tried to eat it. I notice a female figurine hanging from the ceiling by a string. You know the type: a diaphanously clad, long blonde-haired creature, with head thrown back and Barbie limbs, one leg lifted at the knee, barefoot in her pointed toes. Her arms look like paddles—on closer inspection I see they're wings! Outside the door, the telltale shuffling of papers, and then he yells: "Tell her it was benign and I'll see her in six months." Clearly not the message meant for me, and I'm beginning to feel I'm in a foodless diner.

The doctor has that type of beard—there must be a name for it—in which the bristles surround the lips and chin but the cheeks are shaven. He's not about sharing information. He's also affectless, and as for skill, he pokes rather than presses: he gives me the most painful breast examination of my life. I say, "Ow." He says, "Sorry, but it must be done."

"You know I'm sort of considering…I haven't had a chance really to think much…but over the weekend I was mulling and I'm considering maybe finding a woman to perform the surgery." He's just given us the cancer news but now he abruptly rises and literally shows Jean and me the door—an object item I haven't really noticed till he swings it open and flees. He moves through the door and simultaneously mumbles without meeting my eyes, "I'm sorry

I can't do anything about my gender." He also keeps me from having my pathology report. Maybe I can get it in a week, the receptionist tells me, when the part-time worker who does xeroxing comes in—she's awfully backed up, but it will cost fifteen dollars for the first page and twenty-five cents for each subsequent page.

Notice, notice, notice a feeling of being bludgeoned, not by the news but by his affect. But notice, too, en route to radiology to get my records, notice in hospital elevators and sterilizing halls, the feeling of my smiling. I'm joshing with strangers in the halls, I'm almost catching my arm inside the elevator door and laughing, I'm smiling, I'm glad, I'm surprised to feel glad, I understand I'm glad to know now, to have the news, to have enough news to act on, to live with.

Words matter. "We didn't find what we were hoping for. It *is* cancer" was how I got the news. Whereas a friend of mine who had cancer was told, "First of all, I want you to know you saved your own life with your finger; secondly, you're going to be in expert hands. There'll be a whole team of us taking care of you. Third, you might not hear everything I have to say today because it's all so overwhelming, so I'm going to take notes for you as I go."

Since getting the news, I see the world differently, of course. For days I've been noticing beards—they're everywhere!—the kind that surrounds a hungry, pouting mouth and lacks a face.

To read or not to read. That is the question. My new surgeon, whom I find in the ensuing days on the advice of a friend, is amazing. She's generous, informative, brilliant, and highly skilled, and my new doctor is human, by which I mean, in the midst of a seamless presentation on infiltrating ductile carcinoma, she exhibits what they call in poker, "a tell."

She reads breasts and I read people, so I couldn't help but notice her tell. She was walking me through the labyrinth of possible treatment trajectories, a map of logical if this, then thats, and how we would confront each if. She had inspired my confidence like no other doctor in the history of my body outside of Ronald Batt, MD, specialist in endometriosis, bless him, when she said, "*You* don't want to be in the operating room any more than you need to be, and *I* don't want to be in the operating room any more than I need to be. . . ." When she said this, she lifted her hand to her lab coat, simultaneously touching her own breast and pulling her coat across her breast more fully to cover it. I don't remember if it was her right or her left breast that she did this to—my problem being in the right breast at one o'clock as they put it—but it meant something to me. Like ambivalence around the very thing she's good at.

Maybe she doesn't entirely like cutting into breasts.

Maybe she's afraid someone less skilled than she may someday have to cut into hers.

Maybe she likes cutting into breasts and doesn't like that she likes to.

Maybe she thinks I want her breasts, and maybe I do, though I couldn't make them out behind her lab coat and it's her hands I take most seriously. I'm really interested in and mystified by the destiny of her particular hands operating on my particular breast at this moment in the midpoint of both our lives. The fact that my hand writes her that wouldn't have met her if not for this, or would I have? I can't possibly read her tell, but I note it, and find in it desire intermixed with knowledge, which makes her more like me, which makes her human. I don't conceive of our relationship as involving an anonymous set of shes.

And yet the encounter makes me newly appreciate the work of the earlier radiologist who didn't ask me my name. Because I can't imagine the kind of reading she daily has to do, the stakes of her interpretations, the concentration required, the need to distinguish what must, in a day's work, begin to look maddeningly the same. Names might have to fall out of such a picture crammed with yawningly bland or boldly declarative signs, of a lexicon of shadows, peaks, and grey matter, dense or dotted, variegated or matte, perversely amorphous as smoke signals.

In the week of waiting for the news and still hereafter—after "getting" it—my readerly apparatus goes a little crazy. The world suddenly seems full of messages meant for me. Every sign, a harbinger. There are a plethora of signs transmitted mainly through animals and plants. The world abounds with them. While bicycling with my friend, Karen, a swan sails directly over us. When was the last time you saw a swan fly that high? Never. This has to be a "good sign." A rabbit sighting—also good. Meaning: birth. Wild turkeys on the way to the airport with Jean. Standing uncannily in a plot of ground alongside the rushing highway. Regally plumed and puffed just like the paper ones on Thanksgiving tables. We've never *seen* wild turkeys. Indecipherable. Alone in the garden, the wintergreen I was going to pull up—it was decimated—is suddenly abloom with an abundance of new leaves. Message: you too will rejuvenate. Alone in the garden, one of my favorites, the honeysuckle plant, is covered in blight. Aphids, I notice, are sucking the life out of one cluster of blooms, until my eye climbs the stairs of the entire plant, all eight feet of it, usually happily wild in all directions, completely covered in aphids. It's me, it's cancer, I'm going to die.

Is to read the world this way plain narcissism, or more severely, solipsism? It's life reduced to the saccharine dimensions of an O. Henry tale. O. Henry's "The Last Leaf," as I recall it, features a depressed bedridden woman who has begun to identify with a vine that is growing outside her window. Every day, someone opens the blinds to her, and every day, with the season's change, more leaves have fallen, just as every day, she feels more feeble. She's convinced that on the day the last leaf falls, she too will die. An impoverished painter who lives in the same building as she gets wind of her *mishigas* and paints through the night, by starlight, a trompe l'oeil leaf onto the wall to trick her into hopefulness and living. Unfortunately, though it works for her, he, in true O. Henry storytelling fashion, falls off the scaffolding to his death. (Presumably what he "wins" is knowledge that he really is a better painter than he thought he was because his leaf was so convincing).

Imagine if the world could be about something other than ourselves

It's a little sad to think that after all these years of seeing, I can't see the world for what it is, as something distinct from an extension of myself. Honeysuckle bushes don't tell us things outside of how we and the environment make it possible for them to grow.

Post notices. Take note. What's new? Did you hear the news? Making nature into a messenger tells me that I want the world to notice that I'm in it, and to notice, just as significantly, that I'm gone.

Remember a book called *The Secret Life of Plants*? Its author tried to convince his readers that your plants could read your mind, feel your feelings, even register your mood and droop or spring accordingly hundreds of miles away. What could possibly have been going on in the culture to have produced such a book and made it a bestseller? It must have been a cataclysmic, desperate time of people out of touch with themselves and with each other.

Do I believe in messages? Are messages a kind of news? I'll tell you this much: what's really unnerving about aphids on the honeysuckle plant is that I sucked the nectar from a few blossoms the day before—a practice begun in childhood and never given up—which means I probably ingested aphid eggs. I'm not sure if that's good for cancer or not. Are aphid eggs compatible with cancer or a deterrent? I'll probably never know.

For those who believe in messages, here's a tale: coincident with finding my lump a second time—because I noticed it one month and thought nothing of it until I felt it a second time—I dreamt about a woman named Dana. If this wasn't enough, I also saw Dana on a street in downtown Providence the following day. She was strolling with a backpack slung onto one shoulder. She glanced backwards at me, and I almost called to her—"Dana?!"—but stopped myself because Dana has been dead for at least eight years. But this woman on the street had the same butch swagger, the same blue-eyed glance, the same ease of movement, even the same downy blondeness on her neck. The same I had to stop myself from kissing one day when Dana, the sun falling into the window of her pick-up truck, drove me to her house to see her new tractor or her herb garden or new chapter of her newest book. Dana and I were hired into the university's English department the same year, and I was glad at an orientation meeting at which we'd both arrived to find a fellow dyke. With a lump the same small size as mine, and she was only thirty-eight years old, Dana's cancer showed up in other parts of her body and she only lived a year beyond its self-discovery. "Seeing" Dana, I tried to psychoanalyze my sighting with a friend because I don't believe I really *saw* Dana but that I wanted to see Dana, I was particularly missing Dana that day, but why?

Because I wished she were alive to share my new book with, but also because, as I spun explanations with my good friend Arthur, my good friend Karen, my good friend Stephen, it had turned into a repetition compulsion that went like this: *"Don't you think it's wild that I'm inventing this lump in my breast just now? It's so transparent! So much that is good is happening to me this year that I'm superstitiously afraid I'm going to die. You know, I've been so blissed out for so long, and at first I thought my father might die during my book tour, or that my brother might truly attempt suicide instead of checking into the psychiatric ward—he's back to calling me daily this month. So now I think I'm facing the real fear, it always comes down to the fear of your own death, right? These other worries are just displacements. If you die, you don't have to face your desires. It's all so transparent!"* When Stephen hears me talk this way he starts to cry, as though he knows something that I don't. He cries and apologizes, and calls me back and cries some more, and says he's just been in a mood and is sorry he burst into tears.

Dana Shugar, dear Dana, didn't visit me in the merry month of May 2007, nor did she, in walking ahead and offering a backward glance, come to me to invite me into the "beyond." Dana Shugar, one of the healthiest, strongest people I've ever known, was in this case a message I was trying to give myself *to see the doctor*. Dana's meaning: you really should get that lump checked out.

Amid the bustle of the conscious life abloom, there's another active set of selves worth listening to; unconscious. Living is so untranslatable, unbridgeable, even occasionally unlivable in this regard that it daily presents us with messages worth listening to and messages worth ignoring. Here was, as I see it, a message from myself meant to help myself, though at other times, we're nothing better than our own self-saboteurs.

A friend asks me if I'm sleeping, and I say, "Yes," and really I'm amazed that I'm sleeping, that the news hasn't disturbed my sleep. But of course it has because I'm *dreaming*—of chemotherapy sessions and furtive consultations inside of overly tiny rooms. I'm dreaming, which is still better than not sleeping. Maybe the question is: "Are you dreaming, or have you stopped all that?" Maybe if we're dreaming we're still "messaging" and in that way, unlike frightened Hamlet—*"to sleep perchance to dream"*—we know we're still alive.

Now that cancer has announced itself, and I've not just felt but acknowledged its presence at one o'clock, though I prefer "northeast." I fear that it might "travel" before the lump's removed. Will it travel? Is it traveling now faster than the pace at which I place these words upon the page? *"...when I have fears that I may cease to be...."* I imagine if it travels, it doesn't do so on its own, willingly in search of a destination because it's tired of my breast. I imagine it blundering in aqueous nothingness, utterly without meaning in its movement, but this is only because I wish to remain more meaningful than it, for there's every possibility that my body, not just my mind, is a complex messaging system. If the cancer travels, there must be signals involved and even interpretations. For all I know, my life and death are premised on my body's interpretations of itself.

Does a cancer cell sound, and if so, at what frequency does it speed a person to his death? These "signals" involved in cancer's moving—can I turn them off? Dim all the lights? Play dead and trick the cancer into dying too?

These interpretations of the body's relation to itself are neither right nor wrong. I've been telling my students this for years in the context of literary interpretation: there is no right or wrong interpretation, but some interpretations are better than others, and the best interpretations are those that make most possible a new account of truth, a different world, an abler set of options inside the nothing.

～

For most English profs, teaching advanced courses is more fun than, say, the class at the beginning of the beginning, the "introduction to the major," in which students know less than nothing, not even their names or that naming has meaning. Whenever I teach that first course, though, I have the happy surprise of watching another human's eyes widen to what they had never before considered: there's a joy in basics, in ground-breaking, in fundaments. On the first day of class, we talk about the assumptions that attach to English profs—beards and pipes and grammar police—and to English majors. There's a difference between cultivating an alert or loving or inspiring relationship to language, I tell my students, and being a grammarian. We're not grammarians, I explain, nor are we training particularly to become beauticians, morticians, magicians, technicians, or electricians. I give them a new word for themselves; I explain that the power and pleasure of the English major is in becoming a semiotician—a reader not just of books or of literary uses of language, but of signs as basic to living as cells, and just as constitutive of what we take to be real.

Signs tell us how to move in our bodies and at what pace; they tell us who we are and how to know that; they even tell us whom to love and how.

It's funny how there doesn't seem to be a middle ground where semiotics is concerned because once you begin to notice how language represents reality, justifies acts, and becomes a determinant of future action, you can't shut the newly born faculty off. Once you become sensitive to sign systems, you aspire to the multilingual, you recognize in yourself a signer among signs. No longer an amnesiac in the world of signs, you proceed as though ever and always in love: you cling to words, you're a hanger-on of words.

My students and I pursue a double entendre that looks something like this: what does it *mean* to *interpret* things? What does it mean that humans have this interpretive capacity? How can we hone it and later put it to good use at the same time that we never claim to master it, but remain naïve and humble inside a fun-dread house of signs?

The fact of breast cancer in all its commonness is nothing so difficult to navigate as is its cavalcade of typically indecipherable oh-so-well-meant, meaningfully meaningless signs.

In my first meeting with my new surgeon, I was given the pathologist's report as the single most important interpretation in a cancer dossier, an identifying grid that I must carry now inside my wallet alongside my driver's license and my library card. Exiting the examining room, I was given pamphlets describing procedures, cards documenting appointments, and a folder with explanations of treatment trajectories and expectations. I almost didn't have enough hands for it all when the kind receptionist added, "Oh, and this is for you," and with those words dropped an anthropological artifact from an unnamed culture onto the stash. It was an assemblage of words and objects, and possible uses. It exhibited signs of handicraft and care, however paltry, and its predominating color was among my least favorite—pink.

The gift consisted of a styrofoam cup into which was lodged a tiny, no longer than my thumb, figurine, topped with a rosebud. Someone had tied a thin strand of golden ribbon around the pink budlet, from which also hung a message in bold black print that read: "This 'Bottle of Hope' was made just for YOU!"

I felt an instant aversion to the YOU in capital letters—this you that needed special care, that needed bolstering, that might usurp the you you knew as you. I was acutely aware that it was given to me and not to Jean, to me alone and not to Jean and me. On the elevator, I guffawed, then cursed: "What the *fuck* am I supposed to do with this?" I stared down into the cup's lavish interiors to discover a carefully folded, perfectly pink napkin into which the entire ensemble was lodged.

I tried to understand it. I knew I'd need to respect whoever made this gift just meant for me—to appreciate their intentions, 'cause it's the thought that counts. Had cancer survivors prepared the gift, crazy people low on knitting supplies, or elderly women in search of volunteer work who loved the anonymity of good deeds? Knowing that some stranger's dark cancer day would be brightened by all that pink?

Then I noticed that the slender thread of gold ribbon was attached by a *heart-shaped* hole that could barely contain the gift's ironies: doesn't styrofoam cause cancer? Shouldn't a bottle of hope have something in it? Like one's drug of choice? And here I could only feel a little regretful that the only drugs I'd ever consumed in the course of my forty-six years were Advil, Tylenol (I didn't trust generic brands), and a combination of estrogen and progesterone to keep my endometriosis in check. I'd never "done" a single recreational drug—sad admission—in my life; I hadn't even entered the realms of middle-class palliatives like anti-anxiety drugs or antidepressants. Perhaps there was still time. Perhaps now was the time to live more recklessly because that might give me hope: to buy a pipe or snort some coke. To eat some morning glory seeds and watch the world revert to its vibrations.

But this bottle of hope was empty. Empty of substance but not of meaning, for as I examined it more closely, I discovered that the bottle resembled a tiny milk container, which meant the whole ensemble functioned metonymically as breast. If the little bottle stood in for a breast, the rosebud was a nipple. But there was more: the bottle/breast also wore a badge: a pink ribbon barely clung to its surface, wanly affixed with a sticky backing. Were they gifting me a replacement sampler for the breast I might have to lose? Now I tried again: was the lil' bottle filled with the milk of human kindness? And again: could I stuff into the bottle all of the words I didn't wish to hear, and then toss the bottle, rosebud and all, into the ocean?

I couldn't place, contain, or properly receive this bizarre concoction of signs, suitable to no room in my house that I'm aware of, and I couldn't for the life of me surmise what it had to do with my diagnosis to which it seemed irrelevant. Are people with stomach cancer given trinkets? Or how about cancer of the brain, or pancreas, or prostate? What do the men get in the carefully sequestered wards next door? No doubt a brown manila envelope filled with girlie magazines.

The cup o' bottle o' hope makes me feel my fellow females, all pink and daintily doily-ed, are not making the best use of the slender thread of time from which life hangs. So many docile bodies lining up breast/bottles all in a row.

⌒

We think we are closest to the people and things we can touch, but it is also the case that all this rubbing up against one another collapses difference until those things and people we consider most familiar we know least well, unless we make an effort through language to address one another again as though we're first meeting. Otherwise we risk never plumbing so many unplumbed depths effaced by touch.

I can feel my cancer with my fingers. It feels as if it's floating beneath a soft mound of skin, soft as the small of my lover's back. But I have a need to picture it to know it better, as though I need to be able to think, it not just feel it. I need to be able to *read* it, not just "have" it. To see it and hear it to know how to get on with it.

Pictures of the breast's anatomy haven't clarified matters because just when I thought I had it down, having been presented with images of tubes (ducts) and sacs (lobules), I learned that these structures aren't scalable by the eye but are microscopic in size. A doctor's description of the breast's anatomy as treelike—with branches, roots, and leaves—helps, but I still don't get it, and I don't know why the interior of the breast is so hard to picture.

Illustrations of cancer cells remain similarly obscure. So-called normal cells in these pictures look the same to me as cancer cells, except that the center of the cancer cell is darker and by the time it becomes a tumor, it resembles the footprint of a mythical beast: it's all Sasquatch-like and extra toed.

I haven't entered deeply into the annals of literature on breast cancer, but poised as I am at a crucial starting point, as a recipient of the news of cancer in my breast, I've noticed that everything I've found or read about the breast describes it as a "milk-producing organ." Nowhere is it represented as a highly sensitive erotogenic zone; an orgasm-producing receptor; a complex bundle of nerve endings, deferred pleasure and pain; a WATS line to the clitoris. Or are those just feelings I've projected onto my breast that aren't really real? I don't know about you, but my nipples get hard without my wanting them to: the effect sometimes of a word, a look, a rush of adrenaline, or the weather.

Clearly, women's breasts are signs that we still don't know how to talk or feel about properly or fully. Breasts as integral to desire are hopelessly muted by pink valences and rosebuds. Medical illustrators and manufacturers of cancer-consoling rosebuds, alike, might need writers to help them out, because part of the difficulty is that a rose is a spent sign, and a breast is a sign that is glutted and empty at once.

When Gertrude Stein strung together the words "rose is a rose is a rose," she was attempting to re-arouse a host of possible meanings and functions for that lyric icon, that romantic symbol, a sign voided of vitality by overuse, and sapped of signifying power by sentiment. As one of my students once showed me, a simple transposition of one letter in Stein's line restores to the rose its ample bounty: eros is eros is eros. Stein was also, of course, posing a linguistic counterargument to Shakespeare's "A rose by any other name would smell as sweet." Shakespeare's famous line says that signifiers are arbitrary. That something essentially "rose" exists outside of language. Stein, on the other hand, pushes words as signs into a realm of radical autonomy: rose is a rose is a rose entertains the possibility that something essentially linguistic exists outside of things. Putting the icon "rose" into a seriated structure of presumed equivalence (rose *is* a rose *is*) would seem simply an admission of the word *rose*'s petrifaction, but if you read the phrase out loud enough, you can begin to glimpse language's movement, the fact that language never stands still, try as we might to stop it in its tracks. "Rose is" starts to sound like "roses"; "is" starts to gain ascendancy as a noun rather than a verb; verbs start to appear inside of nouns: a rose is arose is arise is arouse. And what IS a rose (is): not only a sweet-smelling flower that grows on a prickly bush, but the spout of a watering can, a warm pink color, the past tense of rise, a proper name, a flower abused by humans who use them as signs in a lexicon of love.

Emily Dickinson re-inspires rosebuds, too—and neither she nor Stein had breast cancer (Dickinson's actual cause of death is still somewhat of a mystery, and Stein died of colon cancer). Both writers knew that rosebuds were bound up not just with a tired language of romance, but with the ineffability of female desire, and with the unrepresentability of breasts in particular and female anatomy in general. Neither negation was acceptable to them, and neither is acceptable to me with my newly cancerous breast.

Dickinson wrote a gorgeously fragmented letter to her sister-in-law, Susan, that I've never been able to get to the heart of even though, every time I read it, it makes my biological heart quicken. The letter is an address on longing in which Dickinson uses the trope of a rosebud to ask, "What is longing's most fulfilled time?" A crude translation of the letter might pose its question as something like: what's your favorite time? Before, during, or after? Part of it looks like this:

Inquire of the proudest
            fullest
Rose   closing
      Triump—
Which rapture—Hour—
            Moment
she preferred
And she [would] will point
            undoubtedly
tell you sighing—answer
The Transport of the
Bud—rapture   rescinded
      To her surrendered Bud
The Hour of her Bud—
      session of
And she will point you
   longingly
fondly—sighing
      receding
To her rescinded Bud
   Departed—
   Receipted Bud
   Expended

It's possible Dickinson's answer to her own question—what is
longing's most fulfilled, perfect, or true time?—is something like:
the moment it is cut off, annulled, canceled. Nevertheless, the letter incites rapture, in which sense, it becomes the transport of MY
bud. It incites an erotics of reading. It helps me to think breasts

and cancer and roses all at once, each a bud where "bud" means a potential, a promise anticipating a form, a sign. Each existing in time, because a disease will "take its course": The body. Flowers. Language. All are heir to time. In spite of the unceasing sway of all those *sc* sounds forcing a tongue to touch the roof, to touch, almost, nearly but not quite, the roof of its own mouth.

I hope that my sharing my news, or is it something one "spreads" as in the Frank Sinatra lyric, led to lots of sex across the land. I know when I heard of a friend's cancer I responded in that self-ishly aggressive way that each of us has at least a touch of. I flung myself onto the bed and bared my breasts and commanded Jean to fuck the shit out of me, to have her way with me, to do what she would with me, to "connect me in places," quoting Stein in *Lifting Belly*. To return me to myself by way of the erotic. To "search it for me." "To correct me." To set me right, discipline me, to tell me how to pleasure her. To "perplex me" and "address me." The difference between my despicable fun and yours is that I didn't entertain immunity. I knew my day would come, whereas you think you're going to live forever. And this sort of holier than thouness that I'm asserting—that makes me want to claim I'm better than you though just as evil as you—goes back centuries in the annals of suffering ennobling one, as though life is one big competition for pleasure in which we all lose, but some pretend to win. I *have* had fun, and don't you forget it.

My favorite line from Emerson, I must remember it: "I grieve that grief has taught me nothing."

A cancer diagnosis changes you in this way: you don't want to be taken for dead. You don't want other people to look at you and read death into you or onto you. I experienced my own cancer diagnosis in the same way I experience grief for my dead. Following receipt of the news, I'd forget about it temporarily, and then feel disarmingly overwhelmed by it as though awash, wading in an ever-mounting wave. It's the way I experience the fact of another person's death—waves of undeniable recognition meeting silence meeting waves throughout a day. And my bed takes on new meaning. There's no good way to lie. If I lie on my stomach with my arm dangling off the side of my bed, my cat might mistake it for an object and swat it, because she must be able to tell that I'm something other than what I was. That I'm heading toward thingness rather than liveness. If I sleep on my back, my bed might become a bier.

There are images I have no control over: arriving in Philadelphia on a recent trip, I listen to two messages from my two older brothers left back to back on my cell phone. I never hear from my brothers both at once like this. Hearing them sidled up against each other in search of me, concerned, I watch their voices waft into their bodies' future forms. I'm trying to take a nap in a sumptuous bed-and-breakfast. I'm alone, and beset by this image of my brothers as pallbearers carrying me in my coffin even though I'm younger than they. Consciously, I know what I want done to my body when I die, and it has nothing to do with Catholic tradition, but memory can be more powerful than present clarity or wish, so I see my brothers carrying me because they carried me in so many ways when I was small. I see my brothers carrying me because I always felt both sad for them and envious when, by virtue of their gender, they were made to carry so many of our dead relatives' bodies in their coffins by their sides. Even if their hands shook, and they were grieving, and their hair was light and streaming, and their knees were bending, they were required to be strong.

That I have cancer is not new, but it's news to me. My cancer is not new; it's old, very old. It's been in me for years and in the world for much longer than that, but now it is announcing itself. What's new is that it is readable. My cancer has become legible. But evidently it's been happening, in its way, silently residing for a long, long time.

A person's cancer is new to her but not to itself, and that's all I can deal with right now: its newness to me, to one who generally despises "new." I've always preferred old. I'm a purveyor of junk and secondhand goods, a frequenter of thrift shops, yard sales, and old houses. Old things have life in them; new things remind me of death.

If someone asks, "What's new?" can I lie and say, "Not much." The world has to be more gentle with me, doesn't it? But I can't tell the world my news so it can know to coddle me. The fellow driver leaning on his horn, the sales clerk impatient with my fumbling for change. So I ask it instead to *bring it on*. I invite its punches and pretend I can roll with them, because I can't retreat. I don't like the idea of not leaving the house, so I smile more broadly, not less than I used to, and I'm a fairly frequent smiler. Smile more broadly not less or the horde might trample you.

Address the trees when people's faces fail you. Notice nature: these trees, like long pointed beards turned upside down, bowing every which way, like bowling pins, vibrating and serene as a Burchfield spruce. Say a prayer to them, like please allow me to remain a part of this. If you're quiet and attentive long enough, eventually they'll nod, *ok.*

Your cat could pose a problem at this time because she knows you well. She knows you're moved easily but don't cry often. One morning in the days just after receiving the news, as I was brushing my teeth, I found myself overcome by sobs. I dropped my toothbrush into the sink and wandered toward my study and my books. I sat in my writing chair with toothpaste filling my mouth and self-pitying tears: "I didn't want to be announcing cancer," I said to Jean, who appeared like the genie that she is. "I wanted to announce my book!"

"You *will* announce your book," Jean said, making me think "enunciate." Nonce. At once. Out loud. Would that a quieter personality had been mine. Would that my book could announce itself. At variance. Renounce. Trounce. Rejoice. An ounce. Recount. A louse. Let loose. Refuse. Bemoan this spoon. Our cat entered the room and stared up from the floor head-on at me, a look that was both concerned and stern, a look that said, "What is wrong with you? This isn't like you. Stop it! Stop it! Stop announcing yourself like this!" Jean thought her face said, "Feed me."

I worry about my cat: I worry that when I'm on chemo, she will no longer recognize my scent.

Desire by definition can't be met. In order for it to be active, it can never arrive. Writing is like this too—you can never achieve your best writing, it's always ahead of you. Consummation is a pipe dream, but it keeps you going. The kicker is that in order to keep desire active, you have to trick yourself into believing that it will find an end. That something or someone will fulfill it even though you know that its nature is to strive but not arrive. Even though its nature is boundless and uncontainable. So the question is if you can truly admit this now. Forced to consider not even the probability but just the possibility that the end of your life might be nearer than you thought, what do you do with the nature of desire? With the former belief that desire will be met, with the well-fed illusion that a sentence will come when you call it, recognize and lick your face as well as that of many others? How do you keep up desire's charade now that you know the end point is *the* end point?

Ephemera. Ephemeral is a beautiful word. This is all ye know and all ye need to know. Across the table of a simple lunch, it makes me want to find Jean's lips with my lips and kiss them. It makes me want to feel my lips with Jean's and kiss them.

⁓

This is not a dream: your hand on my thigh, people in rowboats, oboe and tympanum, your kiss, your hair, this beehive, water lily, sneeze, this braid, this lock, this emerald, gnarled day, these peaks of desire, are real. My name is Mary, and words, as I have always believed, cast shadows, shadows being a sign that they are real. More real, maybe, even, than this tumor.

⁓

When Dana Shugar and I were both thirty-eight, when she was dying and I was living, so many things felt hard to me that she found fun. I'd bitch about something I couldn't deal with, and she'd say, "It's fun." I'd rant about something I was anticipating with dread, and she'd say, "Oh, it's fun." And she made fun of her lot. She invited me one day to watch mosquitoes instantly die the moment they bit her chemo-therapied flesh.

I'm in the garden alone. I'm unwinding the hose and turning on the water and thinking about the face of a student I saw the day before who told me that reading bridged communication between her stepmother and her, so she was buying a book for her stepmother and could I sign it. I was remembering for her a paper she wrote about Gertrude Stein and William James. She was the only student willing to take on the hardest question. She couldn't believe I remembered it, so I didn't remind her of the moments in my office in which she cried because the paper was late, and she was struggling with the sentences, so I told her to read to me what she had written so far, and she stopped crying and did that, and I helped her to see how she could keep the paper going, and all of its newborn questions still waiting to announce themselves— how in answering their call, she could take herself to the end of her paper. I'm reviewing our encounter in my mind, who knows why—because I love her fresh and eager face? because I talked with her at length about ideas the day before but didn't tell her of my cancer—when I'm aware of a presence, soft and silvery, still and fluttering: a dragonfly has landed on the bright white sleeve of my T-shirt, pleasingly poised like a beatitude, an antediluvian grace. This has never happened before! This is new! At the same moment that I notice its unexpected beauty, its gentle eye, I scream.

And it flies off.

Surgery:

measure

I would go back to sleep, and would sometimes afterward wake again for brief moments only, long enough to hear the organic creak of the woodwork, open my eyes and stare at the kaleidoscope of the darkness, savor in a momentary glimmer of consciousness the sleep into which were plunged the furniture, the room, the whole of which I was only a small part and whose insensibility I would soon return to share . . .

—MARCEL PROUST
Swann's Way

prior to apses and steeples and stained glass, and having not yet arrived at the "violet velvet of the evening air," the first fifty pages of Marcel Proust's *Swann's Way* address quivering; a deep or light sleep; and, chance. Proust, I decide, is the best thing to read in the hospital before surgery because his paragraphs can withstand and maybe even require what Freud called, in the psychoanalytic encounter, "even-hovering attention." It doesn't matter if I catch every word; the sentences don't ask me to follow a narrative; words, instead, bob to a surface and also disappear behind it as a perfect accompanist to the buoy I feel I am. I could just as easily have chosen William James or Gertrude Stein for literature-as-science, for the book most appropriate to a hospital setting versus a beach, for reading as an experiment on one's attention, but I chose Proust because one little part was a sign of a voluminous body that no one could master though they might try, and also because I thought of Proust as having a fondness, however exasperating, for infantilism, and in that sense, a license to regress.

Prior to surgery, I had dreamt about my childhood bedroom. If only I could recreate the mood and tone of that dream, I could tap something of the primal within me. "Did you write it down?" my shrink had asked. "No," I replied, "I didn't." I only knew that my mother and brothers were there, not my father, and a tiny bed of solitude. Dreaming of one's childhood bed on the eve of submission to medically induced sleep and operating tables must suggest a return to one's earliest experience of solace *and* terror, dread *and* comfort, as though the thought of excisions and incisions of delicate body parts offered me one last chance to tap and re-master an earliest auguring, something essential that still lay buried, wordless, but that could come in handy now if it could be dredged. Could its transformation from four walls into the scaly skin of a large sea creature and back again to four walls be felt by fingerless eyes and then described?

The first fifty pages of Proust's *Swann's Way* had softened the hard-backed bottom of the gurney where I waited for several hours for surgery to begin. After so long a time, I settled in with my book until sheets became crumpled and the paper surgical shower cap began to lean sideways on my head: I must have looked like the boy who appears happy though sick in Robert Louis Stevenson's *A Child's Garden of Verses*, but without the toy soldiers. "Isn't she a cute lady!" a nurse exclaimed to no one in particular, as though thinking out loud to herself about the latest edition of furry creature in the hospital zoo.

Proust introduced a gauziness into a scene determined to be solid rather than fluid, and later gave me a language for a desire to be brushed up against *rather than entered by* a disease entity. By a feeling. By life, or by others. Because a brush could be more powerful than penetration: a sweeping past that draws forth, a near-touch that presages a deep evocation: a sounding. Someday we will treat cancer with sounds rather than with knives, but not in my lifetime. So I must cling to the conundrum of gauze curtains as if to exigency: open yet closed; thin enough to hear through but opaque; the gauze curtains that separate one bed, one person, one consciousness, one gurney, one situation, one ailment, one anticipation from another.

Through the beige curtains I hear an anesthesiologist ask a fellow patient if he's ever had surgery. "Only when I was ten. I had a tonsillectomy and circumcision all in one go. They got me both above and below!" he tries to joke, leaving me to wonder why he wasn't circumcised at birth. And then he tells the doctor of how honestly afraid he is because his father had the same surgery he is about to have, and he was the same age as he is now, in his sixties, and plagued with knee problems. And the surgery went well, that wasn't the problem, they repaired the knee, "But he never woke up from the anesthesia." The anesthesiologist assures the man that those were different days, as though before-time is always cruder and more ignorant than the moment in which we live. Today the anesthesia is more refined and less likely to compromise major life-sustaining mechanisms. "You'll see," he says, "I'm going to continue this conversation with you in the recovery room." I feel myself twisting and want to yell through the curtain, "Hey, guys! Thanks for adding a little more terror to my own tray of fears! Can't a person read Proust in peace?"

Ah, but so much of Proust is about anesthesia, even in the first fifty pages of *Swann's Way*: I read and mark the lines, "*The anesthetizing influence of habit having ceased, I would begin to have thoughts, and feelings, and they are such sad things.*" Or, "*Just as a patient, by means of an anesthetic, can watch with complete lucidity the operation being performed on him, but without feeling anything, I could recite to myself some lines that I loved or observe the efforts my grandfather made to talk to Swann about the Duc d'Audiffret-Pasquier, without the former making me feel any emotion, the latter any hilarity."* Which maybe explained why my anesthesiologist had read Proust, though I still experienced *his* intimate knowledge of Proust as a surprise. He bows toward me, goggled, with a mildly ghoulishly friendly look, to tell me they're ready, and he's going to start a little bit of a sedative, a mild narcotic into my IV. Nearly instantly, I feel it quicken my heart rather than slow it down—my resistance, no doubt, to sleep, because I want to tell him I'm going to bring into the operating room a Proustian triplet I've just read to get me through. "What's that?" he asks, and I say, "the smell of the tall chestnut tree, the baskets of raspberries, and a sprig of tarragon." We haven't begun our journey yet, we're paused together at this Proustian threshold, when he leans toward me again, like a courtier, and recites his favorite lines from a writer he couldn't possibly know, living in the eighteenth century as he does, and I repeat them back to him.

I retain a sense of the merely brushed but not wholly entered, the emphatic *whiff* of Proust, in the recovery room, where I latch on to the words of the surgeon quoted to me by Jean—"smaller," "less," "only," "all of it," "easy," "see you next week." I decide I've been singled out for *this*: not to *have* cancer, but only *to have had a brush with* cancer, not to die, but to have had the proverbial *brush* with death. To be grazed by the bullet, to feel the furry buzz of the bee at my ear, to sit stock-still while it hovers and not be stung. I revel in my good fortune, but also want to perform good acts as a result as only the chosen and the saved are capable. The scathed unscathed. The whispered to. The spared. To join hands with those with whom cancer has flirted but not married, on whom cancer has cast a spell but not entered. "Oh," I breathe deeply, relieved and released, I luxuriate in the privilege of casting the line of my imagination far because with a tumor so small and (presumably) uninvolved lymph nodes, chemotherapy couldn't be in my future.

I'm not prideful but quiet with this sense of thankfulness inside my tent inside a Proustian encampment. I can afford now to imagine, to be expansive rather than to shrink, so I wonder how the fact of my breast cancer would be treated differently, by what words, glances, food, and sounds, by what rituals or procedures, in what weather surrounded by what smells, in Italy say, where rain rarely falls but drizzles into wisteria's padlock-like flowers, where the right, fresh herb is in reach; or in Sweden, where the car engines purr rather than rattle. On the farm or in the city, what colors would I receive as a healing gift? I'd like to know my cancer in different cultures and parts of the world. I don't want to stop here at the edge of my bourgeois coffee table and the stuffed animal I just received in the mail that I'm told I must bring to all of my appointments with me and then pass on to another sick person when I'm healed. (But I'm *not* sick, remember!) Or the suggestion that I might have to work now on unblocking my energy, and someone can help me to do this by telephone! (But I don't know anyone more unblocked than I and think I really could use some corking.) And the *Watchtower*-like medical illustrations, mannequins aglow in spite of cancer-treatment fire and brimstone. And the offers to "Please let me know what I can do." Or the pink-ribboned paraphernalia, mugs, magnets, T-shirts, and hats. Or the salutations *now* of "love" rather than "best" in e-mail correspondence.

Inside a soaking, crackling summer rain, I mis-hear the word "hysteria" inside "wisteria"—"Look! The hysteria is blooming again!"—and I contemplate the possible reasons that cancer has grazed my cheek, because not to die is to be given a chance, and if given a chance, there must be a reason. I develop a new and sudden interest in Bette Davis movies. As though, given another chance, I should appreciate Bette Davis to whom I never paid much heed. Her signature gestures I now understand as hovering in the space between silent cinema and sound: the demands on an actor to tell with her hands and eyes or to tell with her voice. It's a new on-screen body, wide-eyed renunciation held inside a delicate frame, and it has a crisp and fuzzy halo that makes me think I'm in a dream.

I'm fascinated by this touching-not-touching just now: can we all admit that holding a bird in the frame of your eye is not the same as holding a bird in your palm? I'd asked my surgeon if I could see the tumor when she removed it, though I didn't know how they'd manage that with me asleep. Later she told me they'd held it aside for me to see, but then forgot to show it to me, and anyway, she had marked it by then with different colors to identify its many sides, the way it had been positioned inside. I had felt the tumor but never seen it, or only except as a cornflower on an ultrasound screen, or as a newly formed planet inside the body understood as dappled firmament. In the case of the bird, touching would bring you closer; in the case of the tumor, seeing would. There are no rules.

What makes backstroke so wonderful (but I haven't done it in a very long time) is how it convinces you you're untouched because floating. You're not even looking forward but so carefree you're moving but looking up. Today I ask Jean to hug me back to back rather than front to front. To touch each other vertebrae to vertebrae, tailbone to tailbone, then, rather than say, "I love you," tell each other what we see.

How lucky I was! My anesthesiologist recited lines from Proust to me that were his favorite. They had to do with memory. I recited the sentences back to him and even mused on them before I fell to sleep. But I've since forgotten them. I can't remember what they were. I cannot bring them back. Each gesture and word and Proustian sharing vanished; everything disappeared into the ether, except for the fish-like outline of his goggles that made his eyes look overlarge. If something brushes rather than enters me, perhaps those words will stir.

Backstroke enters my consciousness now not because of a desire for transcendence but because, following a surgery that I thought would be my last on a cancer itinerary but that turned out only to be my first, I had to learn how to sleep on my back for nights on end, maybe even forever, when I had always been a side sleeper and entered into deepest sleep only on my stomach. People who need that belly contact are told to try to substitute a pillow for the feeling of the bed touching their stomachs; positions of slumber have to do with how you preferred to be held in the days when you were still a baby animal.

It's ninety degrees in the shade this New England early summer, only part way into an even hotter because tumultuous twenty-first century, but since my first surgery to remove the lump and a single lymph node called "the sentinel," I've been wearing almost continuously a red-orange corduroy jacket better suited to Fall. "Don't you want to take that jacket off? It's only one of the hottest days of the year," Jean asks, as though taking the temperature of my reality-testing mechanism. "No, I don't; I like it," I say to Jean, and my friend Karen smiles. "Haven't you noticed that she hasn't taken off that jacket since this whole thing started?"

"Thou shalt wear me to all meetings with doctors," the jacket commands. Here's a jacket for all typically frigid waiting rooms. Here's a blanket in need of a thumbsucker. These red-orange corduroy sleeves encase, enfold, engulf, thus nullifying any need to choose between being penetrated or only grazed.

It doesn't work by way of denial but only protection, because when a knife enters flesh, as it now has in my cancer trajectory, when it dares to open what should remain softly closed, responsive, supple, when the scalpel introduces a hairline crevice at the border between the areola and the less differentiated mound of life that slopes toward it, there is no turning back from the fact of *matter*. A body bleeds, swells, hurts.

Cutting and injecting are the culture's modes of care, but while the cutting is obvious and expected, the injections always take me by surprise. Don't ever think again that a noninvasive technology, a procedure as blithely named as "scan" (a brush?), won't entail injection. It always does.

There's no verb in the English language for how a body is forced to comply inside an MRI machine. "Lolling" doesn't convey anxiety's mutations there, though it does begin to broach the ridiculous suspension of two breasts displayed downward into holes cut through a table. You lie on your stomach attached to everything and nothing, to a whoosh of air, to a lit tunnel, dark on either end: you hang onto the movement of your own breathing, knowing if you continue to breathe too fast you'll dissolve. In one hand, beyond the reach of your vision, you narrowly embrace a rubber bulb that you're to squeeze if you can't take it and want out. In the other hand, you hold on to nothing, but are tethered by a needle's painful burning at your wrist that enters you with dye. You lie on your stomach with your head to one side and are commanded not to move for twenty-minute intervals. You insert a body double in your stead because you're not supposed to be here. I can comply with the neon-tinted hammering sounds, a buzzing sledgehammer applied with metronome precision to my skull, and get brainwashed out of anger like the kid in *Clockwork Orange*, or lose my mind.

"June is Interpreter's Month!" a boldly bannered sign with streamers all abounding reads in the corridor between the Gamma Knife room and the underground MRI pavilion, and it isn't referring to me. At first I thought it was celebrating translators of American Sign Language, but then I remembered I was in the halls comprised of silent readers. I never ignore the imprint of the pathologist's name, an electronic signature at the bottom of a page replete with readings. This must be the job you take if you're not a people person but have a yen for medicine. You're not a people person but you want to have definitive effects on other people's lives. You're only answerable to a cell. You can wear sweatpants stained with Sloppy Joes. You can even smoke—and not just cigarettes—in cubicles devoid of doubt. You have 20/20 vision but keep others at the distance of a telescope. Your job is hard enough, and on top of it I want to touch you, even though I know that you're an antisocial geek.

One definition of "interpret" introduces a third term, the interpreter as an agent between two parties. Interpretation is never binary. It's always a bundle, a structure, at the least, a trio, a tryst, making all the more haunting the medical interpreter as a person who's all and nothing but eyes.

Inject me. Reject me. Suspect me. Eject me. Detect me. Ignite me. Delight me. So far, everyone had seemed nice and smart—the woman who strapped me to a table for a bone scan and tied my feet together with a band so they'd point toward each other the way they never do in life, the way I imagine they might en route to the crematorium, was especially simpatico. Only the woman who prepared me for a CT scan of my chest and abdomen struck me as doltish. I'd already, as instructed, drunk several liters of piña colada-flavored chalk on an empty stomach when she informed me that there would also be an injection. This "stuff" she's putting into my vein, she tells me, is going to cause a sudden burning sensation around my throat, abdomen, and intestines. But not yet, not yet, it hasn't gone in yet. It might also give me a feeling as though I had peed my pants, she explained, but not to worry because I would only feel this way, but won't really have peed my pants. To pee or not to pee, that is the question. If this was supposed to prepare me for the procedure, it had only succeeded in scaring me shitless. A horribly weird sensation did work its way in segments from upper body to lower body, as though peppercorns had been implanted at key respiratory junctures throughout the body's pathways. It was as though I'd swallowed a mildly smoldering coal, or as if a tribe of trolls were scorching me with candles of their own devising, culled from discarded wax figurines found in people's attics. All of this was unpleasant, perhaps as unpleasant as peeing in public might be, but the sensation was far from the feeling of micturition. "If

CALLED BACK • 47

that's what it feels like when you pee," I wanted to tell the technician, "I suggest you visit the doctor," until I realized that would
take her to the very place we found ourselves today.

⟿

*"But it was enough if, in my own bed, my sleep was deep and allowed my
mind to relax entirely; then it would let go of the map of the place where
I had fallen asleep and, when I woke in the middle of the night, since I
did not know where I was, I did not even understand in the first moment
who I was; I had only, in its original simplicity, the sense of existence as it
may quiver in the depths of an animal; I was more destitute than a cave
dweller; but then the memory—not yet of the place where I was, but of
several of those where I had lived and where I might have been—would
come to me like help from on high to pull me out of the void from which
I could not have got out on my own . . ." (Swann's Way)*

⟿

It wasn't dementia that I was experiencing in the CT scan waiting
room, even if I did feel as though the child on the TV screen there,
or someone behind the scenes who was moving her strings, was
mocking me. "If you're healthy and you know it, clap your hands."
The girl sang, grinning like the girl in *The Bad Seed*, a macabre,
doll-like smirk, "If you're healthy and you know it and you really
wanna show it, if you're healthy and you know it, clap your hands!"
Clap-clap-clap. "They say I ain't healthy even though I feel healthy,"
I talked back to the television set, "so I guess I won't clap."
    Cancer confers new meaning on the word "disposition" which I
now experience as a verb. Instead of thinking of my disposition as

a stable something that I have, as a mood or personality trait, as in, "You have such a pleasant disposition," I experience a *disposition-ing*. "How are you?" a person asks, and the subject of breast cancer could reply, "Currently, I'm being dispositioned."

People beckon me, certain that it is me they are addressing, but I want to reply, "You talkin' to me?" even when they spell my name and repeat my date of birth. "You talkin' to me?" It's not Robert Di Niro I wish to mimic when I fantasize my reply, but any number of my students over the years. You can look straight into their eyes and ask a question, and they'll reply, "You talkin' to me? Who, me?"

I've lost my position on the map; the chessboard is overturned; the floor is scattered with push pins. I receive calls. On the morning of the day I'm set to find out if *it* is cancer or not, I receive an innocent message from an entirely separate doctor's office where I had recently been tested for the scourge of herpes. I had surmised that the periodic suppurating sores that erupted, of all places, inside my nose, were herpes, but over the years no doctor had confirmed it. The message was cryptic. And prophetic: "Tuesday, June 5th, 9:36 a.m., Hi, this is Dr. Ellen Rose, calling from Women's Health. This is a message for Mary. I, um, got results of your blood work done, so, no emergency at all, everything looked pretty good, *except our suspicions came true*. If you want to give me a call, our number is. . . ."

The day following the diagnosis, my voice mail tells me I have one new message. A woman named Andrea Brown with a strong Southern accent explains, "I'm trying to locate a Mary *H*. Cappello who at one time lived in Middletown, West Virginia. I'm calling from the treasury securities office in Petersburg, West Virgina. And, well," she goes on as if asking a question, "we have some health funds that we'd like to get released out to the right person. Could you please call me back?" Though *cappello* means "hat" in Italian, I am Mary C. Cappello, so I did not call the woman back. Could the H have stood for "health" as in "health funds." Was the recipient's name Mary Health Cappello? If that were the case, the gal they sought definitely wasn't me. *The world is out of joint. Oh cursed spite that ever I was born to set it right.*

In the ensuing weeks, I receive e-mail messages from people who only knew me in childhood. They cannot know about my cancer. They find me while looking for something else on the Internet and want to say hello across the miles and across the years. Across many years and points of no return but of lives whose paths were once the same path deeply hewn in a hollow, not a haven, called Darby, Pennsylvania. They tell me they're proud of me. They ask me if I'm married.

In waiting rooms, there's this same searching and finding, or failing. A sense that you must share something other than a present with your fellow patients: a past that's caused you to converge. If you're overly zealous about cancer's defining power, you could even imagine that the whole point of your life up to now was to meet these particular fellows in these particular rooms. You're kin, but also never called. You're there, alongside of, but invisible.

There's a door in my surgeon's waiting room that is especially torturous this way: I think it's the door to the records room, and healthcare personnel at erratic intervals issue from it while you wait. Each one who emerges is en route to *somewhere*; you feel acutely their determination to points well known, while you bask in indeterminacy. They bolt through the door, but never with you in mind. It's not you whom they're after, whom they call.

Something similar happens each time you exit into the surgeon's waiting room. Sometimes you're in tears and running, but mostly you're above it all—your meeting, after all, with its delivery of good news or bad, untoward findings or pat regards, is over, but you feel all of the eyes of the waiting women on you. These women's faces take on a cast they haven't had since childhood. They search you, readingly. They want to know what you've just learned, the degree and location of your burns, the extent of your scorching, the depth of penetrations, if there's hope or doom in store for them through you—through your ability to have any expression at all on your face when you walk through the door, each of us the me-not-me to the other.

Forgive me for mincing words. I realize all these lines have passed without my having explained that I'd been "skewered." To begin with, on the morning of the first surgery, a radioactive substance was injected into my living breast. I felt it too. This was a method for pinning down precisely the sentinel or most likely lymph node that a cancer cell might travel to if enticed to leave the tumor. From here I found my way to the Anna Pappas Imaging Center, where a guide wire, truly a needle and metallic thread, was inserted into one side of the tumor (see living breast) and out the other. The "area" was numbed but as the doctor noted, I still might feel something as the slender line went in. "Did you feel something?" she asked as she pushed. "Yes," I felt something, and I admitted at the moment of puncture, push, and perforation, I felt a dull pain and pop at the center of my right ear! Such a new feeling, life was full of feelings I'd never felt before despite my middle age. It was like nothing I'd ever felt before that piercing, as though the tumor in my chest was now a lump in my head, and I thought I'd been coping with it well. It wasn't until I got up that I felt the effect of the jolt.

Sitting slowly up, I realized I was shaky and afraid to step onto the floor. The technician seemed used to this reaction and kindly steadied me. She told me to take my time and stood close by (was I holding on to her?—I can't recall). We chatted. She asked me about my teaching and my writing and told me about a niece of hers who liked to write poetry. Her mother urged her to submit a poem to a contest; the girl hadn't felt particularly proud of the poem, but she won. "How wonderful," I woozily inserted, "it's always nice to hear about a young person who likes to write poetry." "Yes," the woman went on, "but she lives a little in the clouds. I'll pick her up for tennis and she gets in the car wearing flip-flops!" I want to explain that I understand the girl's dilemma, to define "absent-minded." "She needs to be absent to one thing in order to be present to another," I want to say, but I steel myself, suppress a whimper, and march, not certain I won't fall, along a corridor to a mammogram room.

I can't really believe my breast will be mammogrammed after having been skewered, but the mammographer explains that I am lucky because, depending on the location of the tumor, some women need to have the skewering and mammogram simultane ously. She proceeds to measure the wire hanging out of my breast (6 centimeters) in order to estimate the amount inside (approximately 9 centimeters), when she explains that all of these procedures will give a "detailed map" to Dr. C.

I'm considering they might be overdoing the cartography; here are fifty replicated ways of finding the same point. Can't I just point to where the tumor is and direct the surgeon's flashlight there? I'm turning the idea of the multiple ways to find a spot inside the body over in my mind—remembering it's dark in there like life beneath the ocean, it's tangled, watery, and vast, and therefore how important it is to pinpoint the right anemone before diving down. All room for error has been eliminated. We can determine what's what and where's where. I'm shifting on my hard-bottomed gurney beneath my infantilizing hat, so out of synch with my smart black glasses, a one of a kind style purchased in Italy last year, when an anesthesiologist passing by says, "You look familiar. Have you been here before? Haven't I cared for you before?" "No," I say, "*I've* never been here before. You're thinking of somebody else."

"Close your eyes and I'll kiss you, tomorrow I'll miss you, remember, I'll always be true," the Beatles crooned and strummed.

My hand rests between my lover's thighs. I am sleeping.

When do I close my eyes? To what do I open them? I close my eyes when blood is drawn, when injections are made, I turn away. But there are things I want to see: sonograms, echo cardiograms, scans of my body, peerings into, without the body itself. I turn my head away when the pre-op gamma ray machine comes within two inches of my face. It must weigh several tons but creates images as light as gossamer. At this stage of technology's game, it reminds me of the first computers whose components required the expanse of several rooms. I turn to profile, and what I see is my lover's profile, craning to watch, following the technician's enthusiastic cue—he *loves* this machine—the journey of a radioactive substance from the tumor to and through the first lymph node depicted on a screen.

I know this profile. I have loved it for many years. I never thought I would be glimpsing it from inside the forced, taut turning of my own body beneath the heavy slab of a gamma ray machine. But I know this profile. I awoke to it in freezing Buffalo mornings decades ago when my eyes would open earlier than Jean's and, instead of getting up, or waking her, I would, leaning on my side, study her profile, and marvel at the fact that I was in bed with a medieval prince. Or her profile on the first walk we took together. We hadn't kissed yet, nor seen each other's nakedness. We had only brushed up against each other in the form of glances; we met strictly eye to eye in classrooms and offices, in movie theaters and at parties where we arrived with men to whom we weren't attached.

I'm misremembering: we *had* touched each other before taking our first walk together, because our first encounter was on a dance floor and thereafter in the ladies room where a dicey confrontation took place along the order of, "You touchin' *me*?" "Was it really *me* you had meant to touch out there?" Now on this walk—we'd somehow extricated ourselves from a large and mandatory graduate student gathering—we didn't dare touch but only brushed up against one another in profile, tentatively, to press flowers into a cuff or into the eyelet of a sloop-necked, bright, white collar. Jean's profile was beautiful but strained; there was reality to this romance and its aimless stroll, because at a certain point Jean desperately needed to pee, and we couldn't find a bathroom. I felt somehow that I wasn't supposed to see her pain so soon without yet knowing her, only knowing how strongly I wanted her, and how right it seemed to slip a flower inside of her shirt, to the point of almost feeling her breathing.

I'm readying myself for surgery and studying Jean's profile because my face is forced to one side beneath a machine I fear might ground me down to ash: I'm inside, and she's outside, and I see in her profile the person to whom I am closest in the world but to whom I also long to be closer, to be more fully alongside and inside of. I know it is the nature of affection that the beloved can never know the extent to which she is loved, but lately I have the feeling that Jean loves me too much. I feel and keep at a distance, the enormity of the pain—a full-faced monster—that would engulf either of us if either were to lose the other.

When do you close your eyes and when do you open them? What do you look toward and from what do you turn away? "Close your eyes!" the CT scan machine commands me not to look into the laser beams that emanate from the arc beneath which my body slides. Open your eyes, not lazily, but because you've been given a gift that could not have been brought to you except for the accident, the happenstance, of being near and far enough from children not your own who play with such creativity and abandon, you can't believe your eyes are privy to their drama, their story, and their frolic, bare toed on the green that faces Tidal Falls in Maine.

Four children of various sizes between the ages of four and eight are led altogether by the tiniest and the youngest who actively invents games for them to play. She's dogged, driven, and deliberate beneath her mop of curls, inside her sleeveless, roomy, home-made denim dress, as she directs them each to somersault, then hop like bunnies ("She loves rabbits," I hear her mother say), to push each other wheelbarrow style, to fall to the ground and drape bellies across bellies, to run like kites outspread toward the water and back again, to round the trees as if tethered to them by May Day ribbons, to pretend to be puppies burying their bones, to pretend to set a table and sip tea. This is higher and greater than eye candy, this window we peer through from the adult vantage of our nearby picnic table, this holy feast of untimed mayhem, panting, then slowed to a twinkling. I wonder if they'll remember this afternoon beside the place where two bodies of water meet in the off season, the only place I know where barnacles and pine needles crunch together underfoot.

There's a lot of picking up and putting down of each other in these children's play, and the tiny one, more often than not, carries the older, larger children. She has an idea now as they wind down, but they never do, to put each of her cousins to bed on a separate picnic table. To pretend to tuck them in till they pretend-sleep, and twitch.

Sometimes our eyes are given a gift like this. "Wow!" I want to say, "Wow! How amazingly beautiful! Will they remember this?" And as the days pass, as I move closer to days on which my body will be opened to be plundered to be healed, I develop a sudden, out of the blue interest in spectator sports. Turning a corner past an amateur baseball game, a local soccer match, a squadron of young football players, I screech on my car brakes and sit and gaze with interest more meditative than hungry, and experience a newly born joy in watching bodies jumping, catching, running—ebullience of the average body at play.

It should come as no surprise then, but it does seem strange, unbidden, when following surgery to my breast, I picture myself dragging myself to my corner, hopeful to pull myself up to meet the next round. Rather than listen to music inside my head, I mentally conjure, in all its sights, sounds, and smells—but did I ever *see* this fight?—a famous Ali/Frazer match complete with commentary by Howard Cosell. Or I think of Jerry Lewis' flabby, flaccid, spastic body inside the ring, face to face with a man in the shape of Godzilla. I remember the loopy hilarity of Lewis' fancy footwork to match his fake bucked teeth, and how he accidentally punches himself in the face, but not before he swings and misses, swings and misses his opponent until he finally bounces from rope to rope to rope in a maniacal frenzy and then, scrawny and lank, accidentally fells both his rock solid opponent *and* the ref.

This must be my mind's way of readying myself for what the body can never apprehend about itself. The unwinding of the sheet, the removal of the bandage, the lifting of the dressing from the still raw skin. And then the bending of my head toward the spot, or a willing of my eyes now toward a mirror replete with the reflection of my body. Sleepy *and* wide-eyed, it feels as though I have a wound above my eyelid, but what I see without yet comprehending is the fact of one small gash above my nipple and a larger, sad, single, thin lip, a line flashing like a red light, *Proceed With Caution*, bright as a pomegranate, shining from within the skin of my barely liftable arm.

This gap, this gash, this gasp.

"I find the Celtic belief very reasonable, that the souls of those we have lost are held captive in some inferior creature, in an animal, in a plant, in some inanimate object, effectively lost to us until the day, which for many never comes, when we happen to pass close to the tree, come into possession of the object that is their prison. Then they quiver, they call out to us, and as soon as we have recognized them, the spell is broken. Delivered by us, they have overcome death and they return to live with us." (Swann's Way)

If, when I had tried to picture it, my tumor sometimes presented itself as an anemone—following the surgery required to remove it from my body, and then some, following another surgery to excise thirteen lymph nodes from under my right arm—I felt as though *I* were an anemone. It was as though I awoke from anesthesia with more than two hands. I was many hands, and they were all searching for the hands of my friends.

The age-old idea of a "laying on of hands" cannot be underestimated because in the interstitial space of cloud remnants parted by mountain peaks, in this space above ground where the air is thin and yet where I also sensed knolls, clay pots, and trees, I experienced a visitation from a group of deceased relatives. My great-grandmother, Giuseppina Conte; my grandparents, John Petracca and Rose Arcaro; my aunts Frances, Josephine, Eleanor; and, in time, my Sicilian grandparents, Ninfa Bottino and Jack Cappello, arrived at my bedside. Not, per se, to "beckon me," nor to emote great heaps of familial feelings, mournfully disposed. They looked at me with faces of concern but also of confidence and ok-ness as they performed a ritual they appeared to know by heart: together they were massaging my feet and my legs.

A mechanical pump was *literally* massaging my legs you might want to note, and read this as a fanciful projection of my droopily anesthetized imagination. But I would say that no matter what truly exerted a healing force on my legs—and my *feet*, I might add again, let's not forget the feet—*immanence* accompanied me that afternoon, and deep know-how. Because, if I may, my ancestors *knew* how to "appear" and they knew what to do with their hands. They didn't reach toward me with crooked fingers or try to lift me into their fold like grim reapers disguised as friends. They merely substantially—I felt so grateful to them!—bore me a visit. Then departed. But entirely differently than the ways they each individu-

ally had departed from the earth, from my life, because those earlier departures broke time's ties, violently, as they moved on and
left the rest of us to drift, whereas this departure was continuous
with time as I knew it, and I felt more acutely their presence than
their leave-taking. In that instant, I understood their presence more
keenly than I did when they were living, and there was nothing
mournful about their leave-taking at all. They did their work and
left it to me to live, confident that I knew how to.

Prior to surgery my surgeon had explained to me the various levels of tissue inside which lymph nodes reside, how she'd have to
access nodes from at least two levels, and how she would then try
to inspect others before and after her actual dissection. She told
me they usually didn't like to have to fool around with the nodes
above the collarbone. Was I hearing her right? She would have to
put her hand inside the wound, she said, and feel these particular
neck nodes; anything hard might augur a cancerous growth and
warrant their removal. I pictured Pip when she told me this, the
boat boy in *Moby Dick,* who is left adrift at a far, far distance from
the ship, and who thinks he sees, from inside the hollow of that
supreme solitude, busy on the ocean floor, the foot of God upon
the treadle of the universe. I don't believe in God, but it occurred
to me that only God should get to do this—to make a perforation,
reach inside, and feel her way around. Surgery and its instrumen-
tality were one thing; the hand of the other reaching inside and
touching things beyond human reach was another.

It was early in the morning of the day after this act, and I had my
legs drawn up to my chest and the back of the hospital bed lifted,

too, so I could stare into the space in front of me and count the minutes before the arrival of Jean. My body seemed to be made up of feelingless bricks, the effect of the miraculous painkiller, Dilaudid, administered in the night, when my surgeon appeared before me smartly dressed and astonishingly awake to a new day of more such work.

"I feel better than I did after the first surgery!" I report stupidly, brightly, and she mildly smiles, then slowly, like a clever ghost, raises her hand to point to the Dilaudid pump. "I think that's because of *that*," she assures me, and advises that I not forget to take the full dosage of Vicodin as prescribed because "We had to do a lot of manipulating of the nerve, and you're going to be in a lot of pain."

Our meeting comes to too swift a close. "So that's it?" I think. "Is that all there is?" as Peggy Lee would ask. And I realize that I'd like for my surgeon to touch my ankle before she goes. She can continue to keep her distance at the far end of the bed. She doesn't have to kiss my forehead or tuck me in, but can't she touch me after all that we've been through?

How unwarranted our expectations are of surgeons! Think of all she has to put to one side simply to *allow* herself to carry out her work. Think of all that she needs to forget in order to be present to the act—never when she wants it to be done but when it's dictated, according to schedule, whether she's in the mood to open the body or not.

It is for this reason, I decide, that my surgeon cannot touch me even though I want her to: because she has gone so deep, brushing is out of the question.

While I was sleeping, she felt the treadle of my being. Why should I expect for her to touch the surface of my skin when I awake?

Oh, my beloved surgeon: I think I felt you in me while I slept. I felt us coming together, and coming apart.

⟡

On the third finger of my right hand, and sometimes, in accordance with weight gain, on my fourth finger, I wear a ring: a piece of geometry cut in silver, this ring in the form of a coiled triangle was a gift to me from the most gorgeous femme I know. Stephen is famous for giving things to those he loves. The moment you admire something of his, he gives it to you. Thus, in the course of a friendship, I have acquired numerous plants—fern, orchids, hybrid geranium, bonsai; a mirror that has been in his family for generations; once, even a pair of his brown-black tortoiseshell spectacles that I wore for several years. Once, to Jean, he literally gave the shirt from off of his back.

It is since forever that I have worn Stephen's ring. I have worn the ring so long that, like a pair of favorite shoes, it has changed its shape in accordance with my body's warmth and movement. Through the ring, I impress my body upon the world like a handwriting, like a signature, but ever with the knowledge that the ring originates with Stephen and a queer engagement with him and with our living, daily, otherwise. There is no one so intellectually lithe as Stephen. No one as full of grace. I love that I wear his ring.

It's the morning of the preparation for a *scan*, and like the good student that I am, highlighter in hand, I read the instructions that have been given to me:

"Bring any recent and related films to your MRI appointment."
Check.

"Bring your current health insurance information to your MRI appointment."

Check.

"To make your MRI appointment more pleasant, plan to wear comfortable clothing with no zippers or metal. Also, do not use hairspray or makeup and do not wear jewelry or a watch (with the exception of wedding bands/engagement rings)."

Suddenly, I'm stumped. Wasn't all jewelry the same to an MRI's eye? What about a wedding or engagement ring exempted its wearer from having to remove it? Was the assumption that *all* wedding or engagement rings would be cast from a metal that wouldn't interrupt the MRI—certainly a strange thing to assume—or was the supposition hinted here that certain bodily accoutrements were just too precious in the culture's eye to ever leave their owner?

I didn't know until that moment that the MRI machine must be understood as a tunnel of heterosexual love. What could be *my* legitimizing anchor there? Perhaps I could take hold with my tongue my fillings and feel alloyed to my dentist who seemed to exert toward me a modicum of care.

It wasn't enough to be cast a far distance from the self by cancer and its cure. I became stalked by a sense of my absence on the culture's rectifying grid. Before arriving at the hospital for axillary lymph node surgery, I need to be registered. I'm on the beach this particular day, but I'm not a beach person. It just seems the right kind of mindless thing to do on the day before my surgery—to stare into the ocean, the place where life on earth began, and sink into the sand, and nap beneath a pile of books rather than read them. The hospital registrar calls me on my cell phone to ask if I'm "single, married, divorced, or widowed." Does this have something to do with insurance, with post-mortem bequeathings, or is it a question about whether I'm "alone"—horror of horrors!—or if there's someone else they'll need to answer to in my name?

I say, "I'm domestic partnered."

Long silence. "Ok, then you're married."

"No, I'm not married," I say.

"Ok, then I'll put down 'single,'" the person says.

"But I'm not single," I say, and she replies, "Ok, so I'll put down 'married.'"

On the morning of my surgery, I'm called into a phone booth-sized office that has the dusty disregard and undressed feeling of a defunct detective agency office, or the kind of place from which you can arrange to have a telegram sent to a far distant land. The woman who is registering me I notice is wearing an obscenely Little Jack Horner-like ring on her *thumb*. "What an interesting ring," I remark, and she tells me it's her wedding ring, but not before noting that I am married too.

"I'm not married," I tell her. "I told the woman who called me I'm domestic partnered, and my partner's name is Jean."

"Ok," she says, "so you're single," a designation that in this context leads me now to picture myself bare-assed and abandoned in the post-op room where I am trying with all my might to hold on to the edges of a bedpan lest I fall into its sadly silver-colored but merely stainless steel oblivion. "So, you're single," she repeats, and then begins to tell me about her daughter, whom she loves a great deal, and what it was like to give birth to her, and how what should have been a perfect birthing experience—she hardly experienced any labor—was botched because something went awry with the cutting of the umbilical cord and she ended up with an infection, and was very ill for quite some time when really she should have been attending to her baby, and she suspects this was the doctor's fault, but the baby in spite of this rocky beginning, grew up to be a multifaceted gem.

I don't know what this story has to do with queer me and my upcoming operation. I only know that I'm not wearing my ring to this meeting because I know not to bring jewelry or much of anything else except *Swann's Way* with me into the chambers of furtive work I'm about to enter.

You have to admire the skill it requires for one pair of human beings to lift the live and heavy body of another human from a bed on wheels onto a stationary hospital bed. I tell the duo that I'll try to help them to move me from slab to slab, and they are grateful but suggest, on the count of three, I just let them do their thing to me, which they know well how to do. On one level, I feel perfectly fine following surgery—this painkiller is amazing!—and on another level I realize that I'm not even capable of straightening the bedsheets by myself, and that walking to the bathroom alone is out of the question. A friend arrives with a bright gerbera daisy in a pot, introducing the idea of a garden onto the windowsill, and with dinner for Jean, and as the hours fall into the deep dark of night, and in spite of the announcement that visiting hours are over, I ask Jean to read to me from Proust.

"Are you following all of this?" Jean asks me after she's been reading for a very long time, and I say, "Not really, literally, but I'm loving it, the sound of your voice and the rhythms of the sentences. I'm really enjoying *hearing* it." Reluctant to be released into the night ahead of me, I pretend to understand that Jean needs to sleep too, and let her leave.

With the subsidence of Proust, there is noise. Almost immediately, a loud, piercing repetitive beeping sound from the pump that is administering my pain medication; loudspeaker static; rollicking laughter; the crash of a pile of silverware to the floor. But as the hours deepen, there is the more difficult, slowly rising intimacy of what I'm not supposed to hear but that gauze curtains can't keep out—the person in the bed next to me, I can hear it, is clicking her pain pump desperately, repeatedly. It's a low, cricket-like clicking, like the sound of someone pushing the elevator button even though she knows this won't speed its arrival, or pushing the button to get a traffic light to change even though she knows the light is timed. The pain pump won't allow for medication to come through except at predesignated intervals, but she is clicking it, repeatedly, endlessly. At various points, in a voice so weak I don't know how she speaks at all, she pages the nurses to give her more drugs, but they blurt over the speaker that it's too early to give her more.

I begin to feel anxious for the woman in the bed next to mine; I begin to learn that she is much more ill than I. I begin to have a sense that she might be dying. Various medical personnel yell at her in the middle of the night. I don't think she's hard of hearing, but I think they think her pain has made her daft, or that her condition has put her at a far remove from them. "We know you're in a lot of pain," they say. "Your colostomy bag isn't producing enough, so we're going to have to go back in and see what we can find." And then they explain that she's also not producing enough urine, that they fear renal failure, so they're going to have to drain fluid by making an incision in her back. Having just come out of surgery with a starting point of relative good health and feeling as diminished as

I do, I can't imagine that, in her state, this woman is going to be taken into surgery. "Oh my God!" I think, "I've got to claw myself out of this bed, tear aside the curtain, and tell those people that this woman won't survive an operation!"

I begin to imagine a wall with life on one side and death on the other, and the pretense of the wall which is really more like a thin line of chalk that can be erased at any moment. I could be there, but I'm here, I'm not there, but I'm close, I'm near, I hear what I'm not supposed to hear, there but for the grace of God go I.

It must be 6:00 a.m. now, and they come and announce as through a bullhorn to a kindergartner that they are going to take this woman into surgery. She doesn't reply, she has no words, and now they say in lower, sacral tones: "We're going to have to take your wedding ring off, ok? I'm taking off your wedding ring now, but I'm going to give it to your husband in just a minute and we'll put it right back on your hand when you're in the recovery room, ok, we're going to put it right back on the moment we bring you back in."

I decide I must be dreaming about all of these wedding rings, which are clearly so much more important than the body itself, than even life itself, and I don't have one. Maybe I could feel this way about my glasses: if they lost them, I'd be ruined. Or about *Swann's Way*. I made it clear to the operating room nurse that I didn't want to lose track of the book, and I understood she had a lot to keep track of, so I didn't want to burden her with making sure my book got back to me after my surgery. She said, "That's ok. Here's what we'll do. First of all, I'm going to put your ID into the front of the book." And she tore off a huge, ugly sticker with my name and vital statistics on it, and pasted it into the front of

Proust's lovely tome. And then she said, "And we're going to bring this book into the operating room with us. It will be next to you the whole time."

⌒

Red fingernail polish in an anesthesiologist doesn't inspire confidence in me, but why not? Nor did the anesthesiologist's use of the phrase to "put to sleep," as in, "I'm going to be the one to put you to sleep today," quell my fears of what it would mean for her to put me under. Does this make her an undertaker? (A term I guess that has to do with the force with which the funeral director takes in hand matters others would prefer to avoid, as in, "We will undertake great things together.") Is the anesthesiologist an undergoer? (No, that's me.) An understander? It's true she'll be standing as I go under. An undertow maker? I think that was it.

She asks me if I have any piercings—any unseen jewelry clipped to my flesh—and my answer is "no": no piercings of clitoris, bellybutton, labia, nipple, tongue, lip; not even a piercing of the conventional earlobe. I didn't have any piercings, but I did have the urge to be fist fucked right now, just before going in for this surgery.

Prior to our going in, my surgeon greeted me in the pre-op room, and as she chatted cheerily about having just seen me in her office not too long ago and here we were again, she simultaneously displayed a pre-op habit: she took off her watch and looped her jewelry, a ring, through the band of her watch. "How efficient," I thought! "I think I'll try this sometime, so as not to lose a ring inside a pocket if I must remove it." I wondered what kind of ring it was. Was it a wedding ring? I didn't think so.

My surgeon's nails are well filed but a little on the long side. I think they should be blunt for the delicate work she has to do, like the telltale sign of a lesbian hand, and that, in order best to prepare me, she should fist fuck me before the operation. She should close her beautiful hand into the shape of a rosebud and sink deep because I'll let her, because I'll trust her. "Go all the way in," I want to command her. And I imagine her waiting until I'm wet and going slowly, patiently, with grace and care and ease. But I want her to be more violent. "More?" she asks. "Do you want me to go further?" And I say, "Yes. Keep going. Go in all the way up to your elbow. Go as far as you need to go to start to feel me. Go far, and I'll show you how much I can withstand."

One-half pound of Castelvetrano olives; one stick of homemade soppressetta (sweet, not hot); a wedge of Fior di Sardegna cheese; sesame-dotted breadsticks; four fresh figs; a handful of individually boxed Torrone, flavored with the essence of vanilla, orange, and lemon; one large bottle of Costa d'Ora olive oil; several dollops of imported ricotta; one package of Perciatelli pasta.

How close are you to your local grocer? I mean, not how many footsteps is she from your door, but how well do you know one another? Lena at the local Italian imports store knows me well enough to recognize the items in my basket as my usual stash.

"You makin' *cena* tonight?" she asks me.

"No, not tonight," I tell her, "these are all gifts for two friends of mine whom I'm stopping to see on my way up North."

"Ah, nice gift you give!" she says.

For a split second, I consider telling her I have cancer in order to explain why she won't be seeing me much now. Lena will wonder where I am when I stop coming in, won't she? In the months ahead when I imagine chemotherapy demolishing my appetite, when I will be forced temporarily to roll in my awning and stow my cooking tools in their drawers rather than have them ready to pleasure and to hand. The line is getting longer behind me while we chat, and I consider that it can't be good for a food business for one set of customers to overhear another customer explain that she has cancer, so I depart in my usual way, "*Arrivederci, ci vediamo, ciao!*"

Two bunches of beets; a carton of grape tomatoes, yellow and red; yellow and red bell peppers; two cartons of blueberries; three summer squash; one wedge of local sharp cheddar cheese; two heads of red leaf lettuce. Near our New England cabin, I organize meals around the produce grown by our local farmer. He knows us as "the girls"—his anachronistic phrase for us. He knows the location of our summer cabin; he knows we're teachers (he didn't do well in English); he knows us enough to recognize us, but our conversations have never run deep, partly because of a conservative streak emitted by both him and his farmstand. American flags abound, he wears Marine corps T-shirts, and he greets us in harsh, loud tones. He mildly scares me.

"What took you so long to get up here this year?" he asks.

"Oh," I offer a partial truth, "we were waylaid this year, but we're here now for a few days, thank goodness, and your produce looks wonderful as ever!"

The farmstand closes at 6:00 p.m. and it's 6:05, "But, for you," the farmer says, "I'll stay open." We're getting ready to pay for our food when he leans forward as though we're in a casino and he's eager to deal us one last hand. "Would you mind if I ask you a personal

question?" he says. Oh, no, something homophobic is about to happen here, I think, and I'm really not in the mood, but for some reason we acquiesce. "Yes, ok, you can ask us a personal question."

"Are you two girls friends or are you, like, a couple?" he blurts.

"We're friends, *and* we're a couple. Why do you ask?"

Barely have I produced my answer when a frantic energy enters
the scene. Our farmer is literally running to close the two large
garage-like, windowless doors that make the stand visible to the
outside world. Instantly, I scan the room for its nearest exit—only
one door in a far corner. Instantly, I imagine the production of a
gun and the sad irony that I won't be given the chance to survive
cancer because I'm going to be killed for being gay.

"Can I ask you another question?" he's practically panting now,
and we say, "Sure" (better than "shoot"), since we obviously have
no choice.

"Was it hard to come out to your families? I mean how did your
families react?" Before I answer the question, I ask him again, "So,
why do you ask? Is someone in your family gay? Is someone about
to come out?" And before he has a chance to reach for the rifle I've
imagined, he leans back from us, as though *we* might try to strike
him, and he says, "Yes. Well, it's me. I'm the one who's gay."

A few minutes swiftly unfold into an hour while Paul—we've
never known his name until now—tells us how much he likes to
dress in drag. He says it's "his way of relaxing," and that he feels
most himself this way. He shows us photos of himself dressed as
a woman on Halloween (the only day of the year when he feels
licensed publicly to appear as himself). "If I lived in New York,"
he says, "maybe I could live in drag and be a farmer. But not here,

not here." He tells us about the years of keeping this truth between himself and his wife, but of not being able to live this way anymore. He wants to meet other drag queens, he wants to meet other queers, he wants to go public. He's nearly crying, he's hugging us, and I can tell he's not hearing everything we're saying because he's so overcome by the relief of what he's said. He tells us he planned to tell us this and awaited our return.

"So now you know," he says.

"I think I know something about how you feel," I say. "It can be so scary." And then I look at him as if for the first time. "Paul—it's so good to meet you!"

"And I'll bet you thought I was just a redneck farmer, didn't you? You'd never guess I was gay, would you? I do a good job of hiding it."

Jean and I leave the farmstead moved and shocked and dazed: By our own conservatism, by our assumptions, by the power of the truth he has shared with us, by the risk he took in telling us. I feel that I've been in just such an epistemic sphere too recently: the shock of the word "cancer," the tears in elevators, the tears in cars, the disbelief. I feel as though I can't receive so many intimate truths in so short a time. I feel the production of truth between strangers all the more possible because I've been made to test the thread upon which life hangs and hope to find it pliable.

Of course I don't tell Paul about my cancer. Not yet. I find myself thinking all night about what he's shared with us, how life is never what it seems. I think about the plying of my trade, the plying of his, and of how impossible it is for writing ever to do justice to a true thing.

To get a cancer diagnosis is to be made to take your placelessness on a map of misreading that no one can fix. There will be numerous misreadings to confront even if your case is in the hands of the finest physicians in the world. A lymph node biopsy was clear, and I rejoiced by spilling wine into glasses we raised to toast. My friend Jim, who was at that time visiting from California, cried so hard his chest was heaving with relief. But, following surgery, I was given the surprisingly bad news that I wasn't in the clear after all: the lymph node nearest to my tumor was found to be full of cancer. It had a one centimeter tumor inside of it, but thirteen other lymph nodes to which it would make sense for the cancer to have traveled were clean.

My surgeon is known for her unerring exactitude and scrupulous care. But in my case, she failed to get a fully negative margin around the tumor, so she had to re-open the already opened wound and go back in. She wanted to preserve the measure of my breast, I understand; she didn't want me to appear mutilated after the fact of her care. And I, too, I had opted, after all, for a lumpectomy rather than a mastectomy. I knew this was a risk, but I never could have accepted it as expected.

What would it take to admit that there is going to be a mangling involved; that the effect of cancer and its treatments is to misshape? And why should the evidence of such mis-measure be erased? A week after my first surgery, I marveled at the equally symmetrical plumpness of both of my breasts. There wasn't even a terribly visible scar upon my darkened nipple. But what I took for proper plumpness had been swollenness, and once my breast began to heal, I could see and feel the depression where the flesh had been excised.

The disease created a bulge, and the fact of that cannot be made to vanish. The disease began to seep—it broke through branches and veins and ducts and channels that had enjoyed a beautiful integrity before it came.

I appreciate my surgeon's wanting to help me feel whole again following her removal of some parts of me. But I also know that living is a constant recitation of partial losses, ebbing daily up to the shore of our being: every act of speech and love and longing reintroduces a rend, a gap, a tear.

As I write this, my cat rubs against the bareness of my calves, barely, nearly, never fully. This isn't merely an effect of her personality—that she's not much of a rubber or a layer into laps. Like so many of her breed, she very rarely makes a sound upon a floorboard, or impresses deeply the ground beneath her, or a body with herself. She only *thuds* when she wants attention from deaf and stupid humans who have no appreciation for silence or for absence, and who cannot accede to steps as soundless, bare, to footfalls' willful disappearance at every step. She's standing on my paper now asking for a glance, a temporary nodding head to head, but I neither want to stop my writing nor encourage her to flee, so I try reading what I've written aloud to her, until little by little, her green eyes close upon themselves, her fur relaxes, and she's asleep.

⌒

"It is the same with our past. It is a waste of effort for us to try to summon it, all the exertions of our intelligence are beyond its reach, in some material object (in the sensation that this material object would give us) which we do not suspect. It depends on chance whether we encounter this object before we die, or do not encounter it." (Swann's Way)

⌒

Having waited long enough on my gurney in the pre-op room, I wonder why the hospital doesn't offer guided meditation, Yogic breathing, calisthenics, a stroll in the garden, or a roving clown, all of which would prepare one better than immobile languishing on a gurney could for surgery. Having waited long enough, I begin to notice an alarming slackness in the hospital personnel. One doctor shuffles, an anesthesiologist yawns, other figures appear to creep and crawl. They're yoked, I understand it, to protocol. They're nothing like the lively, driven, lovelorn doctor figures on TV. They're existentially cool. They're bureaucrats of bureaucrats, or factory workers boxing up mutations. And I labor under my inability ever to remain aloof. What attracted me to Jean was the mysteriousness of her distance, but it wasn't what made me come to love her.

Boarding a plane in Los Angeles International Airport, headed for the East Coast, I read a sign I can no longer read with breezy disregard:

* * * WARNING * * *
DETECTABLE AMOUNTS OF SUBSTANCES KNOWN
TO PRODUCE CANCER, BIRTH DEFECTS, AND OTHER
REPRODUCTIVE PROBLEMS EXIST IN AND AROUND
THIS FACILITY

No one seems to take it in. No one cries out, complains, desists. We must all think it can't be true; we must all think that we're untouched, immune.

Don't ask me to measure the height and depth and breadth of immeasurable loss, because I can't do that, but I am capable of blaming myself for the mistakes that accrue to my cancer. I start to believe that all false readings and all over- and underestimates are something I'm responsible for because—as I can only say a true thing about myself now in a way I never could before—I'm someone who exudes optimism and strength, vitality, energy and life. So much so that I seem to disappoint the Breast Cancer Navigator, a woman designated to help with all the things a doctor cannot address, and there are many. Each time she sees me, she asks disbelievingly, "Are you *always* this upbeat?"

My surgeon didn't go far enough because my exuberant glow must have convinced her that the tumor was smaller than it was. What is the source of this powerful joy? Does it come from me or from somewhere else? Did my body produce its own cancer or was it deposited there? *"And life flows on within you and without you,"* the Beatles strummed and sweetly sang.

The oncologist thinks I can endure chemotherapy at two-week intervals rather than three because I'm healthy and young. No, I want to explain, I look and seem much younger than I am. Really, I'm old, I'm very, very old. And weak.

I realize bit by bit by bit that measure and distance mean everything to a cancer scenario, and that I've been ushered on to the scene without a metaphysical yardstick. In the U.S., we're used to making sense of size in inches, but tumors are measured in centimeters. If my tumor is 1.8 centimeters, exactly how big is a centimeter? "The size of the tip of your little finger" is the answer they supply, but are everyone's little fingers the same size?

I become obsessed with the signifier "extensive," as in "venous lymphatic invasion—extensive," until I learn that this shockingly mammoth word is virtually meaningless in terms of what it tells us, what it can predict on a prognosticator's scale. "Extensive" slips through the door like a Halloween prank to mock me; a snake in a peanut jar, it zags around the rooms of my consciousness, setting off false alarms. "Some" conceals the truth of things with its lil' bit o' honey smile, as in, "You're going to need to have *some* chemotherapy." See me stupidly brighten to the word "some," watch me lasso the word to my wagon for its promise of "not much": you will be blown to smithereens, but only *some* smithereens; you will be hit by a truck, but only by *one* truck. When, truly, do increments apply?

Some. More than none but less than a lot. Better than more. A handful, as in, "May I have some of those M&Ms?" Or, "May I have some of that parsley?" Someday. Someone. Somersby. Sunlight. *"Some day you'll know I was the one, But tomorrow may rain so I'll follow the sun,"* the Beatles sang and strummed. Sing-Sing. Dim sum. Sometime. Someplace. Not now, not here, not now. Somestance. Fort Sumter. A some a long. A measurement: "dosing" as a chemotherapeutic approach sounds like less but actually means more. To begin with, you will have to be measured for your weight and your height to determine how much of the drug to administer, or to determine how much you'll lose, in weight . . . and in height? I fear that I will shrink. In fact, diminishment on every level is what I picture: by the end of chemotherapy, I'll be two feet tall. Or worse, by the end, Jean will be carrying me to sessions in a salt shaker, at which point they will only need to douse me with a drop.

There are things they need to know but don't care about: that I get drunk on one glass of wine; that I can orgasm without being touched; that the dentist gives me the child's dose of laughing gas and sends me home with express instructions to take one-half of one Vicodin rather than two. By the end, I will be ground down to the humpbacked stature of my great-grandmother, so I try to think Sophia Loren: "To what do you attribute your figure?" reporters asked her, and she answered, "Consuming lots of pasta."

Jean and I have never taken vows "in illness and in health," in credit card debt and in credit card debt, but together we empty and measure the contents of my surgical drain, one part white blood cells—think pus, and one part blood sliding with the force of gravity into a tube that's attached to my side. How does Jean learn how to "milk" the tubing without causing me pain? How do I trust her, let me count the ways. Pointedly, through her reading glasses, because she never wants me to be without a dose, Jean times the taking of my medications and records them on a chart. When I can't reach it, she pushes the antinausea suppository *all the way in*.

I'm happy that we haven't measured out our lives in coffee spoons but tempted each other toward infinite extension. What have we freed in each other, and what have we, in the measure of the habits that we have forged together, quelled?

Following axillary lymph node surgery, the world is suddenly entirely beyond my reach. A favorite enameled green bowl is falling from a shelf. I see it crashing from a distance, but I cannot stop its fall. Someone has allowed corn kernels to display themselves like errant blisters in my kitchen sink, and I can't really grab to lift them out of the drain. My mother seems suddenly younger than I in her straw hat and sunglasses as she reaches to prune the honeysuckle bush, but I fear she is trampling the columbine underfoot, and it's I who wish to climb the beanstalk, up, up. Damn the computer cursor that my friend who is helping me with e-mail cannot see even though it's blinking is blindingly apparent to me.

Remember that Broadway musical, *Your Arm's Too Short to Box With God*? I never saw it, but was all the time fascinated by the canny awkwardness of that title. Remember how E. Dickinson unabashedly used the word "cubits" in her poetry? Only she would know how to relay the feeling of a too-full room in America's nineteenth century by drawing upon a form of Biblical measure: to be exact, the distance from the elbow to the extremity of the middle finger.

Never forget your ancestors: the monumental effort that it took for them to get here, and the relative smallness of your life, a tiny flower in an endless swatch of field.

Rise now, onto your feet. Bend your knees slightly and hold your head as if suspended from above. Slowly, gently, turn to profile.

Open your palms as if to play patty cake.

Turn your palms toward each other as if to make a cat's cradle.

Open, spread, the fingers of each hand as if reaching to find a piano octave, end to end.

Play:

Make of yourself a pulley.

Make of yourself a snare drum.

Make of yourself a silken skein.

· 3 ·

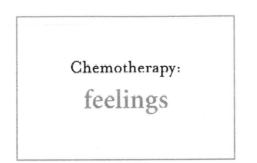

Chemotherapy:
feelings

One of the drugs that I took was an amnesiac, so my memory
of the details of my chemo is very foggy. This is a blessing, and
I hope you are taking the same pill.

—an e-mail from a breast cancer survivor and friend

these are a few of my favorite things, because it's important now to name them: mainly, the way a Sicilian friend of mine Italianizes chemotherapy's abbreviated form: "chemio," she calls it, and how that extra syllable soothes me. Not "chemo" like your MO, like doh-doh, like yo-yo, not chemo like ho-ho, or "Row, Row. . . ." Listen: "chem-ee-oh." But with the *ee* sliding gently into the *oh* the way a bow moves across a violin string, the note before anticipating the one that follows and distinct from it all the same. The way geese skid across the lake, the water now a glissando into which the birds enter, out of which they fly.

Italian, as the cliché goes, is a beautiful language, but this isn't to say I favor a prettifying of something harsh. Euphemisms abound in cancer wards so I don't need really to invent more. An "infusion" isn't a steaming brew of heavenly scented tea but a poisonous concoction inserted through a needle the circumference of which is absurdly out of proportion with a vein.

Like a baby mewling and puking before the naked needle, I

learn, but it takes time, to pronounce first words, names, that were indecipherable to me the first time I saw them, but that soon I came to feel inside my mouth: Adriamycin/Cytoxan. The standard chemo combo for most breast cancers is A/C, and its first member, Adria, is red: no wonder its recipients come to call it the Red Devil. To me, it looks like Electric Kool-Aid Acid. I don't know to what the title of that famous book refers, do you? (I'm an innocent, remember, *suffused* by language). I only know no better phrase for the sight of Adriamycin than a bright red, winking, smiley-face my parents never allowed into the house that was one part water, one part powder, laced with red dye number 3. I'm at a point in my life when I can make up my own mind about Kool-Aid, now infused with a terrorizing jolt and a wildfire bent on putrefaction.

I love the *eeh* in chemio, not for how it softens the bluntness of the thing itself, but for the fact of my friend's enunciation of it. As though her singing it to me with an accent other than my own names it as hers *and* mine; as though in sounding it thus, she hears it going through me going through it. *Eeh* witnesses in a way that *oh* alone cannot: Oh. Chem-oh. Oh. Uh-huh. So what. And Bingo was his name, o.

Someone had told me, but who was it? No one will admit to it now, but I'm sure it was Jack, my analyst, but he said, no, he'd never said this, but someone had, *someone* set me up to think that chemotherapy would make me feel as though I had the flu for a few days out of each month. This is nothing like having the flu, I want to set the record queerly.

The flu is aches and pain and fever, a heightened pulse and a battening down of hatches. Chicken soup, a snowfall, even a blissful suspension for a while. A bug. That your body usually can beat.

The flu in my experience doesn't involve a feeling of evisceration and anomie, as though your inner periodic table has ceased to periodize, as though the key that enters the lock that is an opiate receptor has gotten bent and falls with a clink to the bottom of your brain, as though the matter you took for granted all these years as your body has been replaced by mounds of mismatched Play-Doh, nonporous and salty sour. Note how when you touch it now the body refuses to spring back.

I know this isn't how *you* felt on chemotherapy. For all I know it felt to you as though you had the flu because like you, I've memorized the mantra which my sister novitiates and I say as often as necessary and in chorus: "Everyone is different." No two people respond alike to chemotherapy so you won't know how you'll feel till you feel it.

"Everyone is different" in itself produced a feeling the further I got into the drugs' effects and the more I heard about what other people were suffering. "Everyone is different" was like a political slogan whose only purpose was to remind us that in spite of our having been routinized out of existence by our unquestioning submission to a standardized regime, we were still ourselves!—individuals, democratic monads, unique in every way. "Everyone is different."

"Examine the difference!" I wanted to march through the streets bearing this sign rather than the ubiquitous "Find a cure!" Study the reasons why a friend in Philadelphia on chemotherapy can't walk up a flight of steps this week, while I can ride my bike for miles; while my friend's mouth is free of problems, while mine is full of sores and slime and a surplus of saliva that I call "froth." Study the difference to learn more about the drugs, to free us of the side effects, to delineate the cancers.

For weeks, chemotherapy caused me literally to foam at the mouth while simultaneously, desperately, filling me with anger. Even before the chemo began, though, I found myself beset by fantasies of vomiting. But I wouldn't vomit into my toilet. In my imagination, I would zigzag my way to campus in my car just after a chemo session. I would put other people's lives in danger along the way, and then I'd march to the deans' and president's offices and vomit into their laps and onto their desks. Might this lead them to investigate the building where the English department was housed and the mounting number of cancers among its members of brain and uterus, breast and prostate, lung?

"The administrators weren't to blame, stupid!" I'd remind myself. Their own buildings had been abandoned not too long ago after the EPA found a superabundance of PCBs there. "Alright then!" my anger leaps, "then let's go to the Providence canal on Breast Cancer Awareness night. The entire State House will be lit up pink, and folks will stroll awareness-harnessed to the lovely glow of Water Fire. Let's gather there with other chemonoids and teach awareness as one of us pukes into the canal, another drips tears of blood, and a third keels over, plop, and drowns into awareness from fatigue."

My anger makes me sputter like Daffy Duck, it grounds me down to crude one-liners and makes me want to smash things, following the example of my father who broke all of the furniture in the house *and* our heads when he got mad. "What does breast cancer awareness really make anyone aware of!" I scream at one of my friends. "Ooh, I can see you're dealing with a lot just now," she says, and hurries to get off the phone.

"Feelings, wo, wo, wo, feelings. . . ." The carillon music emanating

from the limestone-clad tower at the center of the campus where I'd started my new job made me stop myself in my absentminded professor tracks and start to giggle. I'd left a position at a school that was private and monied, where faculty enjoyed low teaching loads and research leaves, for a very different milieu, that of the State U, because I cherished my relationship with Jean and couldn't see commuting between distant cities for another indefinite span of years. The chair of the English department at the private institution called me into his office when I told him of my decision to leave. "You're going to take some serious blows in the profession," he warned me. "This is *not* a lateral move!" And for a split second I admit I did picture him as he'd once described himself to me, privy to yet another research grant, sitting in a bathtub for well over a month, doing nothing but reading Melville's *Pierre*, that zany and difficult book that no one reads except for people with research leaves to spare.

I remember thinking, "I've gone from the sublime to the ridiculous," standing at the center of the State U's quad, while the bells rained down the strains of "Feelings" rather than something full of academic pomp. And I noticed differences: classroom interiors that sported cinder blocks rather than wood; linoleum floors rather than carpeting; fiberglass-bottomed desk chairs rather than shock-absorbing cushions for the tush. Almost immediately I became aware that the groups of at-your-service servants at the private university were nowhere to be found here. No research assistants depositing this week's pile of articles to keep you up to date in your field, silently leaving them in your mailbox because they knew you shouldn't be disturbed. No boundless Xerox budget, so most of the materials you wished to give your students you paid for out of pocket at the local copy shop. This was a supply-your-own sort of place—I mean, paper, chalk, even on many occasions, equipment. Which basically meant that, at the level of operations, the university couldn't be an island of difference but a hard-to-penetrate bureaucracy like so many other of the nation's most important institutions. Not a well-oiled machine but a frustratingly persistent paper jam.

Still, I liked it. I loved how "Feelings" ironized academia's insulating self-seriousness. I liked my mettle to be tested. I'd grown up knowing that I wasn't definable by my surroundings (never let yourself be *consigned*). I treated class hierarchies as chimeras and kept my hands busily kneading the essential. I was good at transforming plain old conditions into conditions of possibility. What surrounds you can't destroy you because it can always be transformed. (Note I didn't say "transcended.") I became known for moments when a Nanette Fabray within would burst forth as if from inside a paper drum exclaiming to my weary colleagues, "Hey kids! What this town needs is a show!" So we'd embark on beautification projects, bringing paint cans filled with midnight blue, magenta, plum, deep red into windowless rooms that blinded us with white. I knew that mirrors opened up a room, and took to shopping at Salvation Army for these and for *putti*-bedecked sconces, for low-light lamps to replace the overhead neons, for faux oriental rugs, historic posters and thrift shop oil paintings. (My favorite find was a portrait of Rhode Island's founder, Roger Williams, executed by a woman artist named Rita May Fisk, "Nov 1965," and inscribed on the back, "1 year to dry"!)

When things got me down, I joked. Arriving to mouse turds on my desk, I would leave a message on the department secretary's voice mail with whom I was having a contest: "Today's tally is four. I think I'm ahead!" When black mold overtook my beloved books one early September, black mold on everything down to the paper clips, I posed with the secretaries, making goofy faces behind our masks, feigning fear of the apocalypse. It had always been said of the building that THINGS lurked in the basement. You didn't want to go down there. I could sand down and paint the military surplus furniture in my office and dot my windowsills with oxygen-giving plants, but I remained baffled by weird "remains" that occasionally littered my office floor. On numerous occasions, I'd step into the carnage of an insect battlefield when I opened my office door. Two kinds of insect mutants—they were dead and posed Gregor Samsa-like on their backs—appeared to have done battle with each other in the night. I examined their carcasses and wondered what drew them from their hiding place, what led them to abandon their far galaxy for my office at the State U. Briefly I wondered what substance we creatures great and small both might be subject to, what filled our common air, but I couldn't afford to linger. I had to prepare myself to help my students truly grasp the intricacies of a literary theory, and I wouldn't turn away from what propelled me through the halls. I was busy wafting the off-rhymed breaths and weirdly struck rhythms of the poems of Emily Dickinson.

The only thing that could break my reverie was the pain and embarrassment I'd feel when I'd be forced to witness a brand new brilliant colleague trying to inhabit a truly hideous office. "How are you, Professor B.?" I'd beam, passing by the open door of a scholar sure to become a friend, until I'd be forced to notice that Professor B. was struggling to wipe black smudges—a cross between gop and soot—off of her fingertips, the better to lift her bright, white student papers from her desk. She held a white rag stained black from edge to edge and pointed to her office chair. "Look at this," she said, "I just can't seem to get it clean," and referred me to a patina, no, a thick lamination of grime that clung to her desk chair like a skin. Something was also out of sorts with her windowsill. Its linoleum was curled upward, a long nail protruded at one point, and the cobwebbed insides, dust as thick as bat's fur, were in plain view.

"I am SO sorry!" I'd like to say, "Welcome to the university. This really is a great place and I know we can remedy this."

So I invited Professor B. into my office for a cup of tea. I kept different varieties on hand which I stowed in a beautiful tin, and though it was against state law, a variety of Italian digestifs in pretty bottles.

Some things just didn't make sense, while other details came to light in the course of a decade. Like, I always wondered why the janitors nearly constantly polished the floors while all other surfaces were allowed to accumulate the sticky coffee stains of years gone by, until I learned that the floor tiles were made of asbestos and the U was mandated to keep down any dust that might be produced by our treading on them daily. And the mold? The building had been built on a water table so it would also suffer damage from water gurgling up from below. The building was assembled in the 1960s as an "overflow" site, a place for trailer-style extra classrooms. It was never meant to be lived in as it was now. I wondered at what point it had gained its distinguished name, so appropriate for freethinking English majors and writers: Freedom Hall.

I don't blame my office for my cancer; I don't see the long sojourns there, all those extra office hours spent journeying with students to the edges of existence and back again—because that's what it means to teach writing, to teach thinking—as the source of the endless jog I've had to take with chemotherapy. Like all things in life that manifest definitively—racism, the Patriot Act, a broken toe, this cancer—the latter can't be traced to a single origin; it relied upon a number of forces coming together simultaneously and from different directions in order to appear. My cancer didn't begin in my office on campus: if I really wanted to be patriotic, clearly I should trace it to the six months I spent in Russia. (Or how about the days on end in childhood of eating cereal made of multicolored marshmallows called *Lucky Charms*?) I'm only interested in following the pathways of my feelings out from cancer, and into space; and if I let my feelings lead the way, that's where I arrive. They arrive at the place where I've done so much of my best feeling, so much of my most important thinking: in my workplace.

Here's a siege of feelings, a barrage inside of chem-ee-oh: there's the question of what you'll feel *like* over and against what you'll *feel* (when the feeling truly is beyond comparison and close). The matter of whether you'll feel at all, if you must feel, what you might, could, or should feel, what others will expect you to feel, how you want them to feel, how they make you feel, and how you feel about their feelings. There's a desire—impossible, they say, to know *how* you'll feel before you feel the effects of chemo, and the desire not to feel anything or in any way that you've never felt before.

In medical situations, there's a tendency to narrow feelings down to pain or the absence thereof as though the infinite spectrum of human feeling could be isolated, cut off, reduced to pain's pinprick and controlled. But pain was the least of my particular worries. I was always more afraid of not being able to feel pain than the prospect of feeling it, and I think I have a fairly high threshold for pain.

I think I know how to deal with pain. It's intrusion that worries me. Violation. System overload. Dizziness. Error. It's being yoked to a needle and a drip for hours on end, literally plugged into my chest—it's being trapped, subdued, that hurts. But the thing about chemo, if I want to distinguish it from any other feeling factory that I know, is the incomparable way that it asks a human being to go against what Freud famously called "the pleasure principle": the psyche's tendency to avoid pain at all costs. Even painful psychological symptoms are indicative of this for Freud—they're a person's attempt to ward off something she perceives as *more* painful.

Sometimes I wonder if we humans ever really experience pain, so caught up in avoiding it are we, or if we only ever know it as a specter. Chemo's peculiar tourniquet is this: the requirement to willingly submit to something that *you know will make you ill*. It's the repetition that becomes nearly impossible to endure, as if to say, "Ok, strap me into the electric chair, again!" It's martyrdom without the S/M thrill, it's self-sacrifice with questionable salvation. It's a turning altogether against your right mind and better judgment.

As though my agreement to forge a pact with galloping discomfort were not enough, the chemo nurse made clear that I must each time perform a task to do with feeling. If, for some reason, Adriamycin leaks through a vein, it can cause serious burns to the surrounding tissue. How the veins themselves aren't scorched by it, I do not know, and probably would prefer not to meditate on the fact of the port in my chest's routing the drug nearly immediately into my heart. The nurse's special outer gear when she administers Adriamycin meets you each time as visible proof of the caustic potentiality of the drug. And then there's the sense that the body really doesn't *want* it: Adriamycin is not, like its mate, Cytoxan, administered intravenously, but is literally *pushed* by the nurse into the vein little by little by little by little until it is received. For these reasons, I must tell the nurse *how I feel*—if I feel a sudden pain or burning near the site. This task would seem simple: you're either feeling something or you're not, right? But I couldn't help contemplate how this could be a test that I might fail, whose right answer would save me and wrong answer could lead to irreversible destruction of bits and pieces of myself.

"Was that redness on your chest there before?" the nurse asks after the start of an infusion.

"I don't know," I say, "I'm not sure. Was it?"

"Are you feeling something there, are you feeling differently?"

"Well, I feel a painfulness where the needle is, like usual, but that usually goes away."

"You have to tell me if you feel anything, you know," she repeats with vigilance, concern.

Could I tell her I felt like running? That mostly I felt like pretending not to know who I was? That I felt like turning everything off and slipping off into insanity? I didn't feel anything in my chest, but I could also see that it was red. I felt a little high from the prednisone prep, and rocky headache-like from the antinausea Zofran prep, and hungry as hell for some of the hospital's clam chowder, but I couldn't feel what could be eating me alive.

"Probably a little allergic reaction," I said. "I tend to be allergic to the tape."

And what might my nurse be feeling? Is it safe to ask? I know after the course of several sessions that she most abhors the feeling of putting the needle into and later pulling it out of my port.

I worry about her dream life and the care that she takes, or not, of herself.

Many hours later, rising out of my chemo chair, I wince. "Are you feeling, ok?" my nurse asks, kindly, solicitous, but I experience her sincere concern as a form of disregard. "Of course, I'm not ok," I want to say. "I've been sitting here for the past four hours being injected with chemo and I'm a little stiff! Do you want me to do a jig? Should I stride jauntily to the elevator and wink? Of course I'm not ok, but there's nothing you can do about it."

What I was feeling much of the time was fear of transformation. "How will this drug change me? This regime? This cancer?" I confided to my new poet friend, Deidre Pope, who'd been through this herself. I'd met Deidre through another lesbian friend and only communicated with her via e-mail but told her things I'd tell to no one else. I try to rationalize the change I must confront. "I tell myself that our bodies are constantly changing in ways we're not even aware of," I wrote to Deidre, "simply from aging, from the environment, from how we love in them, from the ways we write with them and teach with them and use them or rest in them." My wishful thinking had a limited application, though, because what's distinct about the change brought on by chemo is that it's drastic. If you have a yen for subtlety, you're at a loss because chemo's reformations are dramatic and totalizing, stupid and raw. "There's nothing intelligent about chemo," I told a former student in a coffee shop, peering from beneath my baseball cap, a little hunched, and she nodded toward her diminished mentor and offered free steamed milk. Everyone is different, but at the molecular level, chemo fails to make distinctions. It doesn't know how.

Thus, you will feel things purely in its wake, violently, starkly. Like hot and cold. Chemo infusions, for reasons not fully understood, can make a person feel, while the drug is going in, teeth-chatteringly cold. Blankets are highly recommended. A premenopausal person like myself undergoing chemotherapy will go into *sudden* menopause, which I guess is better than cardiac arrest, but feels shocking to the body and hot, very hot, as when flashes, so-called, turn your pillow in the night into a smoldering coal. Neither the heat of exertion nor of fever, this heat is both liquid and gas. If you wait and watch for it, you can literally feel it rise till its filled up your entire face, then exits through the top of your head to deposit itself into nearby objects which it infuses with its fire and where it continues to dwell. I wish that I could bottle this heat, or market it.

Feelings of hot and cold create images. Cold: in the middle of the night, I stop dreaming and start to "see things." This evening, a knight in heavy armor, all steely and blue-grey, riding a powerful steed. If romance relied on the knight in shining armor motif, this was the knight in tarnished armor. My imagination, when I used to sleep, worked inside of architectures and gardens, textures and scents, rooms and words, so this unsubtle figure, "cheesy," as my students would say, and overblown, must have been produced by a sensibility other than my own. By chemo? I tried to strike some relationship with the figure on the horse. I felt afraid of it so wondered if I could identify with it, even think of it as me (powerful, invulnerable), until I realized with a chill that this was Death itself, so of course I wanted nothing more to do with it and hoped for it to flee.

Feelings of hot and cold create images. One day the sun, seen through a train window as a glorious ball of fire: heat. Majestic, rare, aflame, there. And the feeling that I can't believe I'm even on

a train while in the throes of chemo, and suddenly a new sensation in the light of recognition of sunshine, of the earth's relation
to the sun, and the sun's relation to velocity, and the speed of my
consciousness, and the felt-ness of my here-ness. Because, for the
first time ever, but maybe I'm a late bloomer and should have felt
this before, for the first time ever, a recognition set me apart from
head to toe from the very thing I was observing. Neither warm
nor cool, neither hot nor cold, this feeling devoid of temperature
was an ache and an acceptance of the sudden knowledge that there
will be a day, many, many days someday, there will come a time
when the sun will rise and the sun will set without me. I felt that it
already had.

What's more profoundly felt? The day *of* a marriage or the day
before? An eve is a corner in time whereas the day of is the other
side of a street. For many months and more, we lived life as a series
of eves: of news, of surgeries, of chemo sessions, of scans. Neither
the day of nor the end of day, the *about to* is where we dwelled. For
stretches, our lives were made of days before. We were consistently
almost but not fully and yet differently poised than the person
about to sneeze, or the person who was just *about to* say, because
those are moments that don't become minutes, those are spots of
time in which you are left behind, whereas the ticking of our eve-
taking coiled us inside a spring that would be sprung not today but
tomorrow, this time of not full knowledge.

I found it best if possible to bike on such days because it was faster
than walking and allowed me to pass. It was easier than strolling,
which suggested baby carriages and thinking, leisurely consuming.
It entailed coasting, occasionally pumping, alerting, and retreating.
It involved bridges, but best of all trestles that foretold of things

safely transported rather than ushered in, and of childhood linger-
ing above a creek, and death-defying dives I never went in for but
only watched. Biking in eve-time was filmic because the landscape
flickered past without you in it, and it wasn't even something to do
in the meantime or something to do while you waited. It had its
own integrity. It was a pedaling best done toward dusk, but without the habit of every evening, because in eve-time it's important
to carry yourself somewhere, not recklessly, but riskily knowing
full well that something will happen tomorrow. But not what.

In eve-time I want to echo a silly Hallmark Post-it note and tape
it to the fridge: "Do it now!" Don't wait until you're sick to have a
sponge bath. Every day should be parsed by such. We should also
walk together more to mark occasions rather than raise a glass or
eat. We should choose a spot and then disperse inside it, bloom. As
on the day I got the news and we received each other with pizza and
wine in Blithewold Gardens. Ok, so food and drink did figure for
us, but afterwards we walked amid wild scarlet roses, many-seeded,
and weeping beeches' leathery leaves. It was early June, and I could
see from the back of his shirt that Arthur was sweating, while Caeli
was outlined in bamboo, while Jean read the map, and I pointed
while Karen trained her camera toward a rush of floating lilies
and the shape of Arthur's shadow vibrating inside a fountain like a
splash. Some flowers were so tiny as to be lost among their leaves,
while others performed in undulating rows cascading downward,
while other kinds were single bursts of pink or white or red. The
perfectness of flowers made the day less wrong. And the fact that
we didn't stay together on the paths but remained open, and no
one cried except to exclaim about a fountain figurine that clutched
an overly fat fish.

As for a sponge bath, nothing can compare to it, neither the rush of a shower nor the langourousness of a tub bath, because it unfolds in parts and increments like the knowledge of your body as you lightly soak it with a sponge soaked in basins filled with steam. The touching and cooling is the best part, and the realization that you have no plans for the evening because the entire day from here on in is made of eves.

Everyone knows someone who "went through it" and is "doing fine," and everyone also usually knows someone, though they don't tell you this, who died of it and is no longer *doing*. I really wish for something other than these crumbs, such crummy language because "it" is meaningless, and "fine" is insultingly inaccurate if not dismissive. A person following treatment for breast cancer will never be *doing* fine, though she will be doing differently. In fact, she'll be doing doing differently. And she won't have done with it, but will continue to attend to it for the rest of her life. The truth of the matter is that no one wants to have to fully contemplate the details of another person's existence. Unless "it" is in a novel and can be kept at an artistic distance and help the reader to feel changed, blessed, and in some way, improved upon—ascending to a finer, higher class (who wants to read a book to be brought down?). I'm not sure a good novel could come out of chemotherapy, especially since for me, so far, it's only produced polemic and invective and some still-to-come *ressentiment*.

"Most essays are finished before they've begun," I tell most of my students most of the time, but I guess I never realized that the refusal to dwell applied to lived experience as well. "You need to stay with your subject longer and let it work on you," I tell my students, but so many of the people who care for me (I mean those who love me) more than anything want my treatment experience to be over. Rather than be with me in it, they try to help me cope with the post-traumatic stress of it before I've even processed it by assuring me that now, thank God, it's done.

No one who isn't going through it wants to contemplate for an instant what it means to lose your hair. Like a hiccough they respond, "it'llgrowback," as though those three words are one, and most of all they'd like to get back to cheering on the Red Sox. Why does a woman undergoing chemotherapy need to explain that *losing* her hair isn't the same as *choosing* baldness as a new and daring fashion statement? One dear friend is so harried by her work life she can only send three words to help me through: "Hair is stupid." This is not to say that the proper sympathy, whatever that might be, is not forthcoming; this is not to complain about the impoverished limitations of our fellow humans' capacity to care. It says something more about a befuddlement around loss even though loss is a fairly predictable constant in our lives. It has more to do with problems we all have in perceiving and appreciating duration.

About hair loss, I had written to Deidre Pope: "I didn't realize how demoralized I'd feel to have my head shaved (the lesbian feminist in me, I guess, I thought would be able to deal with it better). I don't like the way I feel or the way I look with this. It seems to add insult to an already fairly injurious process. Feeling sick on the chemo and seeing its palpable effects makes me more scared of it—and amps up the degrees of trust I'm giving over to the medical profession. I guess this is all to say I feel more vulnerable today."

And she replied: "Feminist or not, hair means something, not only culturally but to each of us personally. It frames your face. It's what you run your fingers through when you're reading or thinking. How can you haughtily toss your hair during a debate, no matter its length, when you're bald? What do you twist around your finger when you're nervous or on the phone? What will your lover pet, tangle her hands in? So, yes, demoralized is a good description. (They say cats are fine if you shave them, except if you shave their heads or their tails. Then they are depressed and demoralized.) It's cold, too, as you alluded to. Who would think to cover their head at night? You just take that level of comfort for granted because you have hair. All of which is to say that it is an adjustment, and not an easy one, no matter what your initial thought was about being bald or how you imagine you *should* feel about it. Because everything you imagine before you start treatment changes with treatment, with the changes to your body, with how crappy you feel, with the anger that might begin to crop up. And then you look in the mirror, and it is now obvious to the world, to you, what you are going through."

Can we take the effects of chemotherapy somewhere, this complex of feelings we're both having, rather than cut them off at the pass, finish them? And once we're finished with them as our well-wishers hope, what shall we return to? Something greater and larger than coming face to face with mortality that formerly gave meaning to our lives?

All manner of treatment pamphlets and cancer center guides, after delineating some of the choicer horrors one might be expected to endure on chemotherapy, assure their reader that "most of these side effects are temporary and will go away following treatment." The temporary works well in bureaucratic contexts—with drivers' licenses and visas, with terms and expiration dates—but where living beings are concerned, temporariness is harder to grasp or to apply. Sure, a broken bone will heal, but will the foot ever be the same, and if it can't, what's the point of saying the break is temporary?

What's well-known but not much talked about is that chemo has both lasting effects and late-developing effects. Given its totalizing violence, how could it not? But even if this were not the case, why should we wish for such a life-changing corridor in the labyrinth that is existence to be forgotten as though it were never passed through? What are the stakes of remembrance?

Politically and practically speaking, remembering makes it possible for one person who's been through it to share information with other people just starting out. If enough people paused, perhaps docility before aspects of treatment that need to be revamped could be replaced by the necessity to question and the strength to resist.

Here's a conundrum: *temporariness* is a human *constant*, if we mean by it the ephemeral nature of all living things. It's funny how we both turn away from the admission that time passes and with it, ourselves—we too shall pass—and insist that significant passages in our life come to an end before we've even experienced them, let alone comprehended them. Is the problem that time robs us of the time it would take to truly live? As though we'd all need several lifetimes to account for being inside this one?

Very early in the experience of my cancer, I felt a degree of pity for myself around a fundamental truth: I had to face the fact that my particular life would have to have chemotherapy in it. That I wouldn't get to live to a ripe old age unscathed by that particular decree. Although I could have, right? Because not everyone gets to a point of having to have this in their lives.

The point of writing it wouldn't be to right it, nor would it be to heal, as in "how therapeutic!" Hobbies are therapeutic, and writing is neither a hobby nor a sport but the place where something begins again differently; more than a record, the writing, an edifice, not an envelope for containing, but a form for passing through, and a shape elicited *from*, words in a match with cancer but not trying to match it, language at variance with the defining matrix of its days. The novel, I now see, would have to be oriented around three seemingly unrelated states: effervescence, evanescence, and recrudescence. It would unfold in three parts entitled, "Time," "Energy," but without the predictable third term, "Motion." Part three would take off from, orient itself around, and seek a language for "Feeling" (e-motion, if you will). In the background, attempts would be made to sustain a drama between the quotidian and the eschatological: a woman going about her daily business of self-care with the minimalist purity of a saint (but really being nothing more than human), all the while having to fend off inherited Catholicisms that linked human suffering with the freeing of "souls" (see winged chariots) from excruciatingly temporary states known as Purgatory. The real challenge would be in finding a way to invest a semblance of authority in the main character, so caught up in backward/forward motion would she be.

At one and the same time, she'd be acutely present to the details of survival *and* entirely convinced her illness and its trials couldn't be happening to her. No sooner would she integrate a piece of her experience into this thing we call a Self, a Voice, then she'd be faced with the self as a mess of scattered pieces and indecipherable sounds, plaintive consonants instead of vowels, ur-sounds—solar, lunar, and plantar—bursts and cries of semiotic collapse. Against her will, meanwhile, she'd be forced back to where "it" seemed to start: with *its* discovery by her, by *its* acknowledgment, by *its* removal. The recurrence of these scenarios would have a comforting effect. The constant repetition in time would make it real, and it would make a difference that other people would appear in these memories as helpmeets and witnesses. Still, in spite of such re-treading, she'd feel left forever with something missing, some unreachable version of a self that went further back even though it had been who she was *not so very long ago*: she could recover her experience but not her innocence. It was the sacrifice she'd have to make in order to re-enter the world. And would that world, re-entered, ever after be experienced as an underworld? The question of the book wouldn't be what she would gain from what she had lost, nor whether language could save her. The question of the book would be a simple "what." Not as in, "What do you want to know?" but, "What are you asking me with that look, without words, what are you seeing?" "What does this want from me"? In relation. What.

I'm five weeks *out* from chemotherapy. In nautical terms, it must be quite a distance from the shore, but my mouth problems persist and I experience what's projected as routine—the surgical removal of my port, for one—as harrowing. In the meantime, I've started radiation. The telephone rings. My friend Jim is calling from California and hoping no doubt for our usual conversation about writing, and about reading, about film, and about politics, but I describe to him the problem with my mouth and the experience with my port until the minutes extend into hours.

"This is so goddamned boring. Jim, do you really want to hear this shit?" If I had any hair to pull, I would, but I don't.

"I want to hear it, yes," Jim says. "I want to know what's going on."

While I'm undergoing chemotherapy, many people tell me that they are praying for me, and some tell me I am on prayer lists. The funny thing about this is that I myself don't pray, but I do make lists. I'm an inveterate maker of lists. I complain when on vacation of being listless. Lists act as simple reminders, as place markers, as maps to guide us through the hours that are granted us, directives that keep us in touch with our responsibilities lest we fly off the handle and *play*, answers to an absent interlocutor's call. My grandmother owned a notebook, the logo on which I enjoyed though I never entirely grasped it: it showed a drawing of a finger with a string tied around it and the motto: "Lest you forget!" I had to have it explained to me that the knot on the finger was a mnemonic device. What I didn't understand, then, was why one would also need a notepad to remember. Why a list? Why not a thread? I suppose the list was called upon when one ran out of fingers.

I'm always surprised to learn that some of my colleagues don't make or keep lists given the myriad tasks we're all made to juggle. I'm convinced they have a secret they aren't sharing with me because they fall silent when any discussion of list making comes up—such a scintillating subject!—as if to say list making is crass, that the list maker isn't living, that lists are like leashes and they aren't dogs. Listless, they are their own masters. "I couldn't function without my list," I say, Lassie-like.

Of course, the nature of a list is such that it never can be fulfilled. Often I lose my list and then have to add to my new list, "Find old list." If I begin to cross off things on my list, I can't enjoy the list as such because it begins to appear too messy to me. Unkempt. And maybe I don't want to think my list making signifies in the same sadly plodding, nearly tragic way that X marks on my father's calendars do. I'll never forget discovering that he had this habit of crossing through the boxes that stood for days on a calendar as each day passed, as if to say, "Finished!" "Gone!" "Gotten through!" "Another one down!" I suppose, "Accomplished!" would be equally sad.

I wonder if I keep lists for the historical documents they become when, after having lost them, sometimes for years, I find them again. "Look at this list I found!" I invite Jean to make a charming trip with me down memory lane as the list remembers for us tasks and trips, purchases and goals, locales, and even friends long forgotten.

Chemotherapy demands lists—scratch pads filled with recordings of how many glasses of clear fluid you consumed daily, descriptions of side effects, reminders around pills and other aspects of a battery of self-care. Combing through mounds of pages of notes, I happen upon other sorts of lists too, telling sorts of self-commands that remind me I'm not just an inveterate list maker but an inveterate preparer, one might say, a fender-offer, in less kind terms, a control freak. Before surgery, I list: "Garden and plants cared for." "Deal with library books." Before the start of chemo, here's a hopeful list of attempts at comfort that I never carry out. Maybe it was more important that I list them:

"Devise a film queue and a reading queue."

"Gather sentences that mean most to me from people's e-mails and type into inspirational notebook." (Had I done this, could it have served as a stand-in for a Book of Common Prayer?)

Chemo pamphlets offer me numerous lists that require rewriting. In place of "You may experience nausea," I'd write: you will feel as though your stomach is an eyelid turned inside out. The stomach cannot receive food with the viscera open on all sides like this, all of its cautions thrown to the wind, exposed, so you may find yourself moaning even if you are generally an exceedingly patient patient. (*N.B.*: Formerly favorite meals may come to smell like burning car tires.)

In place of "You may feel fatigue," try, you will feel as though you are falling through space in an Alice in Wonderland sort of way, but without the security of Dodgson's delightful locutions as safety net. You will feel as though you don't know where your body is, in which case incremental movement may frighten you, but putting one foot in front of another blissfully believing is highly advisable. You will feel disappeared and stony like the marker that will appear instead of you someday, in lieu. Not to worry. The feeling will pass, and you will, like Lazarus, rise again. Very few people die while undergoing chemotherapy, though it has been known to happen. Which is especially sad because such people will not then have the opportunity to revise the chemo pamphlets' lists of how they might expect to feel. And it's important to do this. It's important to remember so as to set the record queerly.

Lists, lest we forget, can be a form of poetry, because what is a poem if not a catalog whose propulsive principle is a recurring leading phrase? A litany that changes some things while keeping other things the same. A repetition that ritualizes whatever it undertakes or takes up: what it lists. A repetition that leads words to shake loose from their moorings and become something other than themselves. Constellations, maybe, or eyes released from sockets. Sounds. A list has no beginning and no end. (I think God was described this way in catechism class, or was it the universe?) A list says I begin in no time and go on. And on. Insistent *and* open. The list. The lines of a list strangely autonomous yet also interdependent. Are lists implicitly elegiac?

"What do you do to stop? What do you do to go on?" I think Gertrude Stein had an aesthetic of lists in mind when she asked such hard questions about habit, about change.

Did list making serve an apotropaic function? Here's a list I found written on, of all places, some scrap as unprepossessing as a Post-it note but with the sticky backing now defunct:

Greatest Fears

- disappearing of all that is important (readings)
- brain fog (writing)
- transformation
- sensory diminishment
- dying before finished my work
- libidinal link

The list has no apparent author. Like most lists, it doesn't need one because it's meant to be disposable, dispensable, forgettable, and unlike high art, strictly utilitarian, instrumental. It wants to be let loose from an origin, it wants to depart from its maker the way a paper airplane comes to rest upon a pile of newspapers piled high inside a door. It does its work and is no more. Still, I wonder why my so-called greatest fears needed to be noted down like this? Was the idea to reduce my fears to chocolates boxed on an assembly line? Here I can take them one at a time; I can pin the live thing down; I can rid myself of the dirty work of weighing, confuse the practical with the ontological; I can type in "fear," then cross fear off.

The problem with lists is that they often rely on shorthand. Thus, I have no idea today what I might have possibly meant by "libidinal link," though a book could be waiting to be written on the phrase. Lists are often private affairs laced with coded language, the self in a dialogue on love with the self. Cancer/chemo fear in the form of a list.

As a child, I used to like to picture a robust Santa making his list and checking it twice, convinced that some small gift would arrive for me whether or not I'd been naughty or nice. Because the list came first in the lyric, before the moral judgment, I rested assured that there must be *something* for me on it. As an adult, in the past few years, I've finally gotten better at asking for what I want or how I want to celebrate a day—a birthday, or holiday. For some people, asserting a want in the form of a list can take a lifetime to achieve. "I think I'd like to. . . ." Fill in the blank. "What I really need is. . . ." "What I've always wanted. . . ."

My lists are always changing. Today's might say, nearly two months out from chemo: "Find ways to coax salivary glands to start up again. Try: lemon wedges? Sucking on."

In spite of this, I mean if chemo is never over, I wonder if it's time for my name to fall off of some prayer lists. I hate to have to think about how my name got on a prayer list to begin with and under what circumstances it'll be cleared to come off.

"What do you do to stop? What do you do to go on?"

The chemo nurse took one look at the veins in my left arm and said, "Yup. She'll need a port."

"So that's another surgery, then?" I asked my oncologist, and she replied, as if to quell my doubt, "The nurses have been doing this for twenty years. They know if you need a port or not."

CALLED BACK • 107

Veins have to be aplenty, and with only one arm available, that's less to draw from. Veins need to be easily accessible—"There are only one or two here I could use." The nurse showed me two faintly blue-green lines on the underside of my left arm. Veins take a beating on A/C, so the port is better all around.

One part silicone, one part titanium, the port resembles the head of a stethoscope, and I wonder how something that size could rest inside my chest without causing severe discomfort. A 30 cm hollow, flexible noodlelike tube attaches to the port. The surgeon manipulates it like a yo-yo string for me to see before inserting. He bounces it inside his palm like a slinky as if to say, "There's nothing to this, this is child's play," or, as I hear often throughout this crash course, "This part's a piece o' cake." I picture moist white cake with vanilla frosting. The slender catheter sliding down my gullet like water through a straw. Or did that phrase linking ease with cake have in mind not how easily something would go down, but how effortlessly a knife might slide through said cake? No doubt it was shorthand for "It's a cakewalk," but the cakewalk, as I understand it, is not particularly easy—though it's possible it was performed to *mimic ease* to white audiences by labor-bound black ex-slaves.

The port rests below the slender catheter which loops *above* it, the better to slip into a major artery in the neck. The surgeon will begin by grasping the vein through a separate incision in the neck. But it's slippery, as I understand it, and no mean feat to grab if there's a pulse moving through it. That's how I understand it as the surgeon dictates what he's doing—"It's a slippery one!"—with me awake. A friend of mine who had her chemo administered intravenously told me how she tried not to look when the Adriamycin went in because she swore if she did so, her vein would try to move out of the way of the needle, it would try to resist the intruder and move aside. With a port, you don't have that option. It's sort of the difference between swallowing and glugging.

"Another surgery." I sadly turn to Jean. "There's always a new surprise! Ok. I can handle it. Watch me deal with it. Only five minutes have passed. I'm already alright with it. See? Ok, I can do this. It can't compare to what I've already been through. I have no choice, right? So now I need to arrange to have a port installed. I'll be portable!"

It was summertime, we were tanned and bare armed, we were sandaled, I had hair, not a single white hair at forty-six. I liked that fact, but something was solemn and unswerving about the prospect of a port.

"Turn away for me now," the nurse said, as she prepared to insert the needle into the port. Going in was one sharp push, taking out was one swift pull. Always she prepared me: "On the count of three."

"Ready?" she asks me, the way Italians answer the telephone, "Pronto! Ready!" and then she'd count: "One. Two. Three!" Months earlier, my surgeon, too, told me there was no better way to remove the postsurgical drain from within my side than for me to take three deep breaths on the third of which she would pull the drain altogether out. So many times now, on the count of three, I cross a threshold of catastrophe and come out alive. I brace myself *and* release myself. I gurgle under water and simultaneously come up for air.

Wherefore on the count of three rather than two or four? Why not just "Hip, Hip" without the "Hooray"? Why not begin the joke, conversely, "Knock, knock, knock," instead of "Knock,

knock"? Or how about, "On your mark, GO!" without the middle term, "get set."

Everything happens in threes was a famous superstition, or was it *good* things happen in threes, or *all* things come to those who wait?

On the count of three establishes a coincident being in time because most of the time we exist at different speeds even if we together adhere to conventions that govern pauses in speech, paces of words, a give and take of conversation. Physically, humans might appear always to be moving at fairly similar speeds (holding to one side the very old and the very young), but at less visible levels of our being, we move at different warps and woofs not entirely dependent on whether we've drunk our morning cups of coffee.

A needle in a port can't be removed on the count of two because it takes at least two beats for the person being acted upon to learn the length of the interval that will precede the final act: "Three!" Three, a glyph originally made of three horizontal bars only later linked to form the number as open loopty-loops we know today. Three produces the conditions of possibility for a relationship between two; on the count of three instigates synchrony and duet. As a disciplinary mechanism, three counts can incite the romantic swelling of two people sweeping across a ballroom in a waltz. Or the bracing fear and heady indecision of a person on the other side of a door: "We're coming in on the count of three!" Or the other side of a parental slap: "I'll give you three seconds to do what I said!"

A duet is beautiful, but a romantic triangle is more interesting. That's why we love reading Tolstoy and Henry James. Who wants harmony when they can have the allure of tension? Inside of capitalism and the oedipal, the triangulation of desire makes love (and money making) tick. Triangulations of desire make the world go round. I want you more if I know someone else also wants you. I never want the thing in itself but the competition with another for it. What a sad state of affairs, in more than one sense of the word, when the beautiful infinitude of human desire is reduced to a competition for mommy's love, no, daddy's love, no, mommy's love. Where rivalrous threesomes win the order of the day.

It's obvious that Three Stooges are better than two, but what can compare to the chemistry occasionally achieved between theatrical pairs? Fred and Ginger. Lucy and Ethel, because even though she loved Ricky, there was no chemistry there, no possibility for the contrapuntal, no mutually rapacious kindling of a spark. Starsky and Hutch. Cagney and Lacey. What could compare to the violently bristling love/hate match of *The Sopranos'* Tony (James Gandolfini) and Carmela (Edie Falco)? Were you as shocked to learn as I that Edie Falco acted for one whole season while undergoing chemotherapy for breast cancer? How did those two maintain their chemistry with her chemistry entirely off? Such duos actually *do* spin on the beat of a third term: us. Our viewing of them.

I have known people who partook of sex in threes, but they refuse to talk about it. As though it was a mistake they'd rather forget, a taboo, though crossed, better left un-broached by thought or discussion. *"We three Kings of Orient are. . . ."* Who could make sense of the enjambment at such a youngly caroling age? "Bearing gifts we travel afar." Or for that matter, who could decipher the idea of a three-in-one godhead, the so-called Holy Trinity: Father, Son, and Holy Ghost? The third term seemed hardest to me since a ghost was different than a spirit, but it was addressed as both, and it took the form of a bird, in particular, a dove. Inside of which lurked "the heavenly host." God's body? The son's? My edible or oedipal own?

What part of God or of me was the Trinity's third term, the Holy Spirit? I know a nine-year-old genius who says she wants when she grows up to marry a parrot and give birth to birdlike kids.

All in good time. Everything in its own time. Does an overarching principle determine the speed at which things move, or are velocities independent of each other and haphazard? Do particles move at one rate while turtles amble at another? I imagine cells speed around, rapidly reproducing inside said turtle while its muscles barely move. My treatment, *on the count of three*, poises me inside an interval, forcing me to contemplate *the time things take*, situating me as a being in undiscovered time.

Between eating one caramel and choosing to eat a second or a third. Between contemplating doing something and deciding to do it. Between a foot tapping the gas pedal and the car moving. The door bell ringing and your opening the door. Or do you simply decide not to answer it and leave the act incomplete?

How long does it take for a streetlight to change, and what do you do while you're waiting? What is the time between paragraphs and words?

How long is the lag between your being touched and your beginning to feel something? How wide is the interval between your receipt of a letter and your comprehension of it? Your purchase of a book and your reading of it? The preparation of a meal and the eating of it? How long does it take to hear what's being said?

How long will it take for seeing to become perceiving, or perceiving, seeing. How narrow is the gap between chewing and swallowing, between waking up and rising. For you?

Between your finding someone beautiful and your telling them so, or do you never tell them and fail to complete the act?

What are you waiting for when you're not in waiting rooms; how long are you willing to wait?

Since receiving my cancer call, like being drafted, because I have to report nearly constantly now, and take orders, and salute, my sense of timing in social situations is entirely off. It's as though I no longer have time for phatic communication. "Hi, how are you, etc." I simply cut grotesquely to the chase. "Hi. I have cancer." I even leave out "My name is Mary and. . . ." Sometimes I tell people this before I shake their hands. Throughout chemotherapy, I cope, I suppose the way most people do, by projecting myself into a better tomorrow (which also puts me in a quandary around all those years of training myself to live in the moment). "Tomorrow, I'll feel better," I tell myself as a way of dealing with feeling miserable today. But what I learn about the chemo process is that in its quivering wake the immune system goes up and down, so the achievement of good feeling doesn't unfold in a straight line of better, better, and better. It's more like better, bad, extremely bad, good, ok, bad again, better.

"Exactly how long does it take for the chemo medication actually to leave the body?" I ask my oncologist. I ask her this because I'm beginning to feel neurotically like a ghost is living inside of me. I begin to feel that I need to be exorcised but I don't have the means. "It takes twenty-four hours for the drug to entirely leave your system," she explains, "and fourteen full days for the body to recover from its effects." (In most chemo scenarios, a third week is provided between sessions to regain strength and composure, but in the "dose dense" form that I underwent, the sessions are spaced exactly two weeks apart.) "Fourteen days for the body to recover," my friend M., a year and a half out from cancer treatment rolls her eyes, "so how does she account for the other energy-less three hundred and fifty one?"

When I was a child, I achieved unbeatable thrills inside the experience of track meets. I loved the feeling of being catapulted by a set of signals in triplicate. One particular announcer would begin by addressing us at the start of a race: "Runners!" Dead silence ensues. With that word we are equalized, we are exquisitely ground down to our capacity for speed. "Take your mark!" And I ground my tiny feet into the grey mulch that was the gravel, held. I looked ahead. Then listened for, from this particular announcer, not the typical, "Get set," but a piercingly attenuated "sssseeeeettttt," each syllable rising across the space of several seconds, winding us up, each sound of a phoneme drawing my back leg up to ready myself to spring. "Go!" would be accompanied by the sound of a gunshot into the air above us as if we were ponies spurred on to flee the crack of a whip, as though we were Pavlov's dogs. I loved the feeling of my body being captured inside this set of timed commands. It was exciting to agree to being held and then released with all one's might. I loved the feeling of outrunning the pace of those commands. In my runner's guise, I learned what it meant to be quick off the mark without ever being guilty of a false start. Submitting to counts of three is different. It makes me feel penned, like a bull, when I'd rather be let loose to run and roam upon a field.

I punctuate my chemotherapy sessions with visits to a tremendously caring acupuncturist. "You're going to see me go through lots of transformations," I say in our first meeting, putting up a shield, knowing that together we're going to see me morph in ways I can't even imagine, ways of which I am afraid. Alice doesn't reply with words, but looks at me kindly. She invites a space of evanescence and indeterminacy. As if to say, "Let's see, we'll see, but now we're here together. Now. And, what's your name?" Alice slows me down so much it makes me want to cry. Midway through a session, I'm astonished. Astonishment. Midway through a session, every molecule of my being achieves an utter stillness that isn't death, a quiescence that isn't acquiescence. Something my acupuncturist has done takes me there, and I hang out there, splendidly alone, floating, enlightened temporarily too.

Unbidden fantasies rush in. More than once, the image of *something happening to me*, an episode interrupting this stillness, the need for an ambulance, and my being driven away. Daily I move through difficulties deliberately, even with extraordinary calm, but in waiting rooms I begin to feel woozy. Am I going to black out, or do people's faces seem pixilated because of the neon lights? I can't keep up the pretense of dailiness, of timeliness clocked by a slow rising and predictable setting of suns. I'm living in a state of emergency, and an ambulance should be arriving *pronto* to take me to some far off hills away from hospitals. Because ambulances aren't all that bad if you compare them to hearses. Ambulances speed, while hearses creep slowly, too terribly slowly, along.

On the count of three, tell me: am I going into or coming out of a trance?

Nobody speaks of loss of pubic hair, but it goes, too, it goes first, leaving you with the body of a Kewpie doll, or suddenly, overnight, a girl. Nobody talks about sex, as though it's expected you just won't have it or won't want it, but I think they're thinking of heterosexually driven male-dominated sex that women don't want even when they're feeling well and wanting sex but not that kind but they endure it. If you type "chemotherapy and sex" into Google, you'll find this: answers to men's repeated queries about whether they can "catch" chemotherapy by putting their penises into their wives' orifices while they're sick. I try to imagine Suzy Sexpert or Annie Sprinkle, Diamanda Galas or Karen Findlay, advising *me*—by all means try to orgasm more at this time, do all that you can to love and be loved. Intensify. Or don't. Try to imagine unsexing, herald Lady Macbeth's command, "Unsex me here!" Resignify. Let yourself be rubbed up against, grain or no grain.

The person who, in an attempt to be hip to the moment of your baldness, DOES NOT invoke Sinead O'Connor should be given a prize. What kind of prize? A diploma of unconventionality. A wisdom beanie. A "You, doll, are one in a million" badge. This would be the person who speaks a foreign language inside the one the rest of us speaks, sans articles. How would conversation proceed differently if you both admitted that you weren't happy sexy bald but chemo bald? In place of "You look *like* Sinead O'Connor," they'd have to say, "You look shorn." Alliteratively and truthfully they could say, "You sure do look shorn." You look *like* you're in treatment for cancer would be where the exchange would begin, only after which it could be said, you look *unlike*. You look unlikely. How does that feel?

"*Che fatto caruso,*" my local Italian grocer, Lena, belted out, as though she were singing an aria, and, in fact, I didn't know this word: *caruso.* So I thought she was asking me who made me into Enrico Caruso, me with this black turned around baseball cap looking awfully attractive, looking defiantly male-like, daring to look like a famous high-foreheaded, olive-skinned, sweetly singing

Italian man. Later I learned that *caruso* is a word for "boy." When did you die and go to heaven and become a boy? Why are you trying to look like a boy? What the fuck is wrong with you? Don't you know you're a woman and not a boy? "Hee, hee, hee," a friend of a friend in the grocery store sniggers, evidently delighted with a revelation he's having. "You look like the little boy in *Bicycle Thief.*"

"You look like yourself, more yourself than ever before. You look quintessentially Mary, bald."

"You look like a monk."

"Ooh, you butch, you'd better run! You're driving me crazy with this look," a gay male friend tells me.

"Mary, you look like Foucault."

"Your head is perfect! Perfectly round. No dents, knobs, or protrusions. You look better bald than you do with hair."

"According to the direction of your whorl, you should be straight."

On a windy day, I feel as though the door now carved into the space at the back of my head just above my neck has flung open. The very place in Chinese medicine, my acupuncturist explains, where illness enters in. Yet another tradition locates a significant chakra at the top of the head, which feels, when hairless, terribly exposed. Early in my treatment, in a waiting room, sensing my trepidation, another woman, a stranger, invites me to feel the flesh under which her port resides. "Do you want to feel it?" she asks, and I do, and it makes me feel I'm at the opening of a cave barely peering in, such intimacy. At the moment of my hair loss, you regard me stripped of dignity in a way I will never see you. "That's not true," you might say, "you can't know that." But I'm talking about now. Can we admit this? Why should you get to see me naked?

Though I do wear hats and wigs, I don't hide my chest flesh and kind of enjoy the fact that I still have cleavage, but my oncologist mistakes a lovely plunging maroon number I wear one day to chemo for a "port shirt," her words: "Oh, you're wearing a port shirt today," she says. She thinks I've dressed for ease of chemo access versus leers.

In Catholic grade school, from which my body hails, I wore a plaid wool uniform in all seasons, day in, day out, and clasped my hands regularly in obedience and in prayer, but I never felt disarmed by the uncanniness when the fingers of one hand met those of the other, the divining mystery of the self touching the self, as I do now. In time, following one week, two, of hairlessness, I begin, through the experience, to know something profoundly elemental. To touch one's own hairless head—if all your life you've never done it—is to touch something essentially inside/out about yourself. It's to make contact with some scarily fundamental you-ness like the place where you first were attached and then broken from a source: the last time a skin brushed your bare head like this was when your infant pate, all delicacy and force, pushed its way out of your mother's body. And there are other surprises: when my lover touches or kisses or licks the top of my head, I experience it as a turn-on. Overnight I've discovered a new erotogenic zone.

A rush of air creases my baldness, like parting my hair if I had some. I reassemble. It's not even real, this whoosh, but an image from a story that a friend tells to me at chemo. She's just back from a seaside town in China, and she tells me about watching photographers there produce artificial wind to make their subjects' bridal veils appear as though they're floating. A great many times my head is stroked without my seeing the touch's source. I *think* my cat is in the room, but she's not. It's this type of absent presence that plays perpetually around my head like the sound of other people's crinoline rubbing against itself, moving. It's soothing, it's out of reach, it's the body in space surrounded by a hushing while some procedure is carried out, it's the sound of someone adjusting the sheets and the faintness of a radio voice heard through earmuffs.

My hairdresser, Jon, before and after shaving it, washes and massages my head with such thoroughness and care. I feel him anoint my ears and forehead; I feel him draw his hands like lavishing combs across my skull, gathering the bunch of me at the back of my neck until I relax and scatter and let him catch me up in bubbles. My physical therapist jumps onto the wide platform in the shape of a bed on which we work, and suddenly she's kneeling behind me like a playful figure in the sand who has fallen out of a *Beach Blanket Bingo* volleyball game. She's massaging my underarm from behind, serious about the business of extending my range of motion, and it's embarrassingly ticklish. My acupuncturist feels for my pulse. It's "slippery" she says, or "damp," but I feel her fingers like the pads of a clarinet bearing softly down on openings to make a sound. She bends to tap a needle into my lower abdomen, an area that's noticeably ticklish when I'm nervous. It's only the seat of the Dan Tien, I note, site of balance, breath, and awareness in Tai Chi—I guess from a Tai Chi point of view, I'm ticklish at the center of my being. I don't know what's more difficult for me: the first time I take my hat off in her presence, or the first time I undress for her my previously cancerous breast. She offers me ginger sweetened with plum juice to quell my nausea; she asks me if my feet are cold and cups her hands to warm them; she shows me how to warm the edges of key pressure points when

I'm at home; she drapes a dressing made of silk across my body and atop my silence.

If my nerve endings are numbed, this doesn't mean I'm no longer *feeling*. This is what my port surgeon fails to understand. I still feel awake to the port's removal, the boom of the surgeon's voice, the enthusiastic timbre of his instructions—he's surly, he's cranky, he's sure—to cut through the old scar at the midline. His assertion of insertions and removals. Local anesthesia does nothing to nullify dread, to cancel out knowledge. The surgeon calls upon a "mosquito needle" to apply the numbing agent, but I feel something more akin to the bite of a blackfly, or a tine test whose prongs I can't see but feel going in one at a time, two times, three. He calls the interns to gather round to catch the sight of something beautiful: the leathery pouch the inside of my body has formed to accommodate the port. Resistance is ugly; acceptance is sublime.

"You have a worried look on your face," he says at the start of the surgery.

"I'm concentrating," I say. "Just getting ready."

"Your feet are tapping. I can see them," he says. "What's going on?"

"Well, hmm, my feet are tapping?" I work to stop them.

He turns the closing of the wound over to the intern once the former, rubbery, stubborn sutures that held the port in place inside have been clipped and then removed, once the catheter has been slipped out of the neck vein, the catheter grasped and the vein pressed upon to prevent its spilling, once the port head has been lifted from its space inside the body.

"Is it out yet?" I ask, picturing with unsedated vividness the hole in my chest, picturing what would happen if I got up from the table now and insisted on going home. "Not yet," but once it is, the surgeon stands to one side and describes a meat dish other than turkey he's planning to make for Thanksgiving dinner, while the intern, I can feel it, patiently sews shut, not a turkey carcass, but the cavity in my chest.

"I can feel what he's doing," I say, my head straining to one side. I feel a lift, pull, pierce, lift, pull, pierce of skin in succession. I feel a freezing drizzle of something liquid dripping across my chest and under my arm.

"More anesthesia!" the surgeon pushes.

"I don't want any more," I wince.

"I'm in charge here," he bellows. "Give her more!"

There are always women in such rooms, stroking a head, holding a hand, reading a face. In an earlier room, months earlier, to have the port installed, sedation *was* involved, but it still didn't numb me. The nurse looked the way the word sounds in Italian— like the Madonna *Dolorosa*—the woman of sorrows, Mary of the *Pietà*, making me wonder just how wracked with discomfort my face appeared, and then at a strategic moment, she held my hand, we squeezed each other's hands for quite some time.

I participated with the surgeon during that ordeal in the hubbub of an intellectual conversation. His ability to talk about my work with me—a book I was writing on the pioneering laryngologist, Chevalier Jackson—in between orchestrating the intricacies involved in installing a port was amazing. I tried to enjoy our mutual attempt to mute the reality of things in themselves even as I writhed, and in this sense, of necessity, performed the opposite of intellection. Not a marriage of true minds but the impedimenta of distraction.

As I rose to sit up, having earlier joked that the operation would render me "portable," I felt heavier than ever. I felt the weight of the little bauble lodged inside my chest tipping me to one side. My teeth chattered so fiercely, and the rest of my body in turn, that I might have been no more than a wobbly deck of cards, or a pile of loosely woven boards swinging between one side of a mountain pass and another. I think I was, as the saying goes, in shock, but I knew I had to compose myself to journey to another part of the hospital for my first chemo treatment. "We'll take you there in a wheelchair," a kind voice explained, but once we arrived, I quickly sought permission to walk to my chemo cubicle. I concentrated on achieving the upright posture that I knew distinguished me as a human being in the world. I felt the need to assert my own capacity for willingness, my ability to walk myself there, to *transport myself*. It was like learning, and how well do we learn this, to smooth one's own bald head, like learning, and at what point does one learn this, to insinuate oneself as a form of self-comfort?

"I could see you were thinking, you were thinking too much," the nurse had said to me at the end of the procedure to install the port at the same time that she admitted she gave me a higher dose of sedative than "normal." I think she was trying to tell me she could see from my face I was worrying, but she used the word "thinking" in its place. I don't remember thinking, though I do think I was heeding and attending and wondering, which might also be different from worrying. I think my nurse might think that thinkers are people who worry, that to think is to worry and to worry is to think, and that people who *think too much* don't do as well as others in situations like these.

Perhaps the problem is that a worrying face and a listening face and a thinking face all have in common a furrowing of the brow. Either the face doesn't calibrate states of mind with enough precision, or the face reader isn't a literate enough discerner of the crinkled workings of a face. Thinking people don't always look serene: when I think hard, I can look like I'm in pain, but when I'm worried, I look like I'm demolished. Worry stands still while thought moves through. A worry is a rubbing that doesn't produce a hard-on. A thought is a flowering of mind. Worry is hardwired where thought is co-creative. Mulling combines the two. Worry is a relative of wear—it wears things down, including hair. Worrying can make a person's hair fall out. Thinking and hair seem totally unrelated, except that culturally, we expect our finest thinkers to have beards, and an idea is sometimes figured as a thing that sprouts like shocks of hair.

"I've been thinking of you." "I can't stop thinking of you." "I was thinking about you." "I think highly of you." How much more desirable than, "I'm worried about you." "I worry about you." "You worry me."

"Think me." "I think you." These are relations between humans that don't yet exist where "think" implies a form of love we're not used to making.

"Don't bother me. I'm thinking."

It wouldn't make sense for a stranger to begin to hold your hand because she thought that you were thinking. "I could tell you were thinking." Stroke, stroke. No. Thinking is something we do alone. It fills its own need even if we need others to enable us to stop worrying enough to think.

The port surgeon and I weren't thinking together—"Think me." "I think you."—even though we each appeared to be tossing around our intellectual weight. We were trying to engage in witty repartee when, as the doors of the operating room swung open and with his coat tails flying, he entered the room. "The last time you saw me," I grinned, "I had hair," trying to deflect my embarrassment as my cap slid off. "Don't complain to me!" the surgeon closed the thought down. "*Your* hair will grow back, young lady. *Mine* will not."

I fold my pajamas after shedding them. I tidy. Things. I empty the dishwasher. Sort recycles. Prepare lunch. I "hydrate" (which turns out to be a full time job). These are the action verbs that orchestrate my day, signifiers of my abilities while on chemo.

One woman holds a dust rag in her hand; a second holds a drink (hard liquor barely diluted by the clink and swirl of ice); a third holds a book. The first two women's houses are spotless, though it's hard to see things in the second woman's house because the shades are perpetually drawn. The body of the second woman is stiff and loungy, cool; that of the first, droopy and tense, at war with the idea of the girdle its owner is ambivalent about donning. The body of the book-holding woman is voluptuous and rangy. Woman number one suppresses a cough, while woman number two coughs a good part of the day, while woman number three sings. The first two women were my best friends' mothers; the third woman was my own, and this is how I experienced them in the thresholds and doorways of my youth. My mother performed her share of self-sacrificing housework—cooking daily for five, washing and then hanging all of our clothes (no dryer). She even vacuumed. But my mother neither "kept house" nor accommodated her body to domesticity's four walls. She wrote: "While I was writing poetry yesterday / dinner burned. / Tony said, as he surveyed his portion of burnt chicken, / "Mom, why is it all day long you sit in thoughtless wonder / then when it's time to cook, / you write poetry?"

My mother read, and it took a lot of time, it took a lot of energy. My mother wrote.

By all accounts, I "do" extremely well on chemotherapy. My ability to exercise daily, to fold, empty, tidy, sort, to hydrate, put me in a tiny subcategory of women on these drugs according to my oncologist. What I cannot do during this time is read and write. "You know, this idea that living is great no matter how you feel so long as you're alive," I tell my analyst, "doesn't suit me. I don't know what living would be without reading and writing. What? Am I supposed to survive on the smell of newly mown grass and the love of others with my drool cup by my side? I'd rather die. I'm not saying I'm suicidal. I'm saying that if I'm rendered incapable of reading and writing, I'd rather not live. I don't want to be kept alive at all costs."

Another part of me, on chemotherapy, is dead set on what I call "substitute pleasures." If I can't eat, I'll have to find something to yield a comparable pleasure. If I can't read, well. . . . For all intents and purposes, I appear to have energy for the duration of my treatment's weeks and months (I go for walks, I water my plants, I "do" e-mail). But I don't have or have access to whatever is required to read, to write. I know of women who can't get out of bed at this time *and so read novels*. The asymmetry is something I fail to understand.

I am able, I am no longer able. These are weighty phrases inside the circumscribed annals of any life, each life a play of flecks of light caught and then extinguished inside a matchbox. On some chemo days, my perceptual apparatus seems hypersensitive: tiny sounds greet me like a crash. I can barely manage the energy it takes to register the sound of my own voice. Films, otherwise known as moving pictures, are out of the question—there's too much going on to take them in.

"I can't believe you're giving readings and traveling," my friend M. assures me and then offers me an image to which she more than once returns: "I felt as though my brain had shrunk *to the size of a pea*." Which also apparently made her afraid during her chemo-therapy treatment to venture out of doors.

"Chemo brain," they call this, also "cognitive deficit," and they say it can last for God knows how long. "We call this an-ti-ci-pa-to-ry anxiety." My oncologist talks to me as though I'm senile. She must be trying to be sensitive to possible chemo brain when I tell her that for the first time in my treatment I am experiencing side effects a few days *before* my infusion. For all intents and purposes, I don't appear to have chemo brain. I remain so piercingly articulate at public talks I've agreed to give I scare myself. It's just that I cannot read or write. I can't be present to reading, to writing's exquisite demands.

Reading must be akin to eating, I decide, and writing, to preparing a meal. Reading requires listening, hearing, extending into the space of another consciousness, stretching toward the invitation of limbs. Words-as-energies I temporarily can't take in. Curiosity. Openness. I never escape into a book, but I do leave my body in order to take on the mantle of a new one. I let a writer teach me how differently to breathe. We read and write to interrupt the daily tale we tell ourselves. The tale that drains us, hopelessly unrevised.

To let the record player needle screech and skid, to come to a standstill, pause, begin again. I read to begin again, and this takes energy.

Perhaps chemo didn't tamper with my energy, a modern concept, but with my *humors*. Maybe I wasn't able to read or write because my *desire* was somehow thrown off course, another modernism. Was this my libidinal link? Chemo, anyway, isn't only a life-savingly, depleting drug regime but a powerfully enervating *discourse:* It's the language of chemo, its narrative expectations and demands, its pink-rimmed salutations, chat rooms, and journalistic jingo, its pamphlets and protocols that exhaust one.

I lift a hand to remove an ingot as if to recite the secret phrase that will unseal the opening to a cave. I bring down tomes otherwise unopened on my shelves—on chemotherapy, I look through picture books. Nightmares had beset me at the outset: of pulling dental floss out of my throat to the point of gagging; of dredging up a *large* bone and piece of meat; of teeth falling out in great number. How could it all come up through my throat? How could it *fit*? I gave myself soothing dreams of peering with Jean into the insides of a Cornell box, of looking through and finding unused rooms. In real time, I summon my might to consume a piece of chicken. Simply, a corner of an (organic) "chicken nugget," but a nibble translates into the feeling of having eaten an entire bird: my stomach feels filled with several drumsticks, wings, dare I say, numerous breasts? I muster the ability to walk around the blocks in my neighborhood in the early evening of the day of a treatment and ask Jean if she's seeing the same thing: I mistake a trash can lid for a pith helmet, an overturned leaf for a bingo chip. Sinking into bed, I can't open my eyes for their tearing, but I hear the translucent *ssshhh* of the pepper shaker, the clink of a tine, a hammering of garlic from down below. How strange! I feel as though I'm holding on to the bill of my baseball cap to keep from falling. When I do eat, it's more like *putting food in*. A phrase I once encountered in a book about a man who died of AIDS.

Pictures replenish me. For a period of time, I eat paintings; I live on reproductions. For every book, a host of memories, so I receive each image as a tiny host, a bit if not a bite. *Masterworks of American Art from the Munson-Williams-Proctor Institute* returns me to Utica, NY, though I'm steeped beneath a coverlet in my front room in Providence, RI. Jean and I had traveled with my mom and her partner, Sid, through the Adirondacks and on to Montreal, then back to Rochester via Utica where we found this museum in which we wandered as though we were inside a woodland, slow and awe-fully, reverentially glad for the fact that not a single painting there could be linked to its creator. Rambling in this museum— we were driving a Reliant not a Rambler—had to be about something other than the viewers' authority in recognizing something "great" because the paintings here were distinguished for falling outside of each "great" painter's *oeuvre*. A town called Schroon, a B&B bathed in the color red, the return to a restaurant forty miles away when I realized I'd left my purse behind, my practicing Tai Chi lakeside before our days began. I was twenty-nine years old and the guided meditation my teacher called "The Inner Smile" made me weep. I was twenty-nine years old, and thought of Mom and Sid as elders, but they zoomed around the Canadian city while we slept. "I thought you were a married suburbanite!" a fellow lesbian in my Tai Chi class let on, "when I saw that car you drive with the fake wood paneling." I switched the blaring music off and bore down on the brakes with both of my feet when this same car's gas pedal got stuck on the stretch of highway that linked Philadelphia to New York. "This is it," I thought. "This is how I'm going to die." But I didn't die, and Sid came to meet me, and they towed the car. I wish Sid were here now. At the same time I wouldn't want him to have to know that I have cancer. I wouldn't want him to know that his son died too soon after him of cancer of the brain. I'm not glad Sid's gone, but I wouldn't want him to know all this.

So I page my way through the movements of Americans making art. I have energy for still pictures, nothing more. People had proven they could learn to talk again, but could you learn a second time to read? For days on end I savored only punctuation marks; I was brought up all over again on color and line. Simple woman and complex landscape, lengths measured in rods. Raphaelle Peale's carving a jugular vein into a head of lettuce and shoving a carrot into a hunk of meat. A horse and his groom. Falls not steppes. Closing my eyes, I see the wardrobes of my caretakers as palettes. The paintings you love when you're well probably aren't the same as the paintings you love when you're sick, but whenever I make the rounds of modern art in American museums, I find myself returning to Marsden Hartley, and it's no exception here.

The painting that holds me best and most is titled *Summer–Sea Window No. 1*, and through it I experience pieces of a landscape as comfort food. If this painting were a recipe, it would instruct the cook to bring to a *shimmer* rather than a simmer. "If it's beauty you're after, hide the roses inside their leaves," the painting says. "If it's a view you need, consider looking through a *baffle*." Because all of its planes are equalized, no part of this painting's scene is privileged, and yet two elements in its arrangement appear to be in competition for my gaze: off to one side, slender, tall, a bunch of roses emerging from a vase; and at the front center of the painting, weighty, thick, a book. The book orients a view of (seemingly edible) clouds and a boat through the window—the book as ledge rather than ledger.

Where do you have to be standing to experience the dock as a desk? What's the true center of the painting?—a book, a boat, or a rose? The book is rose colored, it's saturated pink, and as such is not a book at all but a block of color, an outward form, a surface for reflecting roses. Just as a painting can't be opened, neither can this book, and since I can't read anyway, I drift. I sip some water, keen to tally another glass put in, and drowse toward what I think I can recall: Hartley had written an essay on Emily Dickinson. Was it possibly the first critical commentary on Dickinson's work I'd ever read? "Alone and in a circumstance. . . ." "This world is not conclusion. . . ." "The name of it is Autumn. . . ." Scarlet. Resumption. Crimson. Surcingle. Vermillion. Contusion.

Pang. Heft. Husk.

Propitiation. Blush.

Incautious. Acorn. Dimple.

Twig. Pluck. Wrinkle.

Asterisk.

Seam.

Asterisk.

Elysium.

Asterisk.

Well.

I drift toward tidings, beginnings of something greater, something still to come.

When a glass is smashed to pieces, we usually don't call the window repairman to glue it back together. We're forced in such cases to replace the whole thing. I sometimes wish that language could work this way because it seems so often demolished and unfixable, even though we keep using it to express ourselves as clearly as we can, and most sincerely.

October's magazines in the year 2007 in my city are filled with signs of our breast cancer times; mobs of people carrying torches to brighten the gloom of an evident dystopia; portraits of women, yearbook style, with their age of diagnosis, date of diagnosis, and date of recurrence if there is one. Some portraits are accompanied by inspiring quotations in boldface, such as L., age thirty-eight, diagnosed in 1999, rediagnosed in 2006. A prominent oncologist's words appear alongside the photo: "L.'s beauty, in the midst of chemotherapy, exemplifies her true inner strength." L. is one of those lasses who looks not just beautiful but gorgeous bald—her hoop earrings, perfectly arched eyebrows, her almond eyes. I'd guess her scars, unlike the rest of ours, are sexy. It's important that L. have her beauty going for her on chemotherapy because, as I always like to say, it's not how you feel but how you look that counts. So long as you *look* good.

Think "beauty" while on chemotherapy. That's the ticket. And if you don't look beautiful hairless and retching, anemic and frothy, yeasty and bloated, achy and with that metallic taste leeching out of your back molars, "ashen," consider this a sign of a failing. Not just any kind of failing. Consider it an emblem—our doctor used the word "exemplification"—of an essential flaw, an *inner* weakness.

An entire century has passed since Nathaniel Hawthorne

devoted his life to debunking an epistemology (inherited from the Puritans) of inner essences readable through outward signs. We no longer abide the assumptions propounded by phrenologists and physiognomists that were later used by eugenicists, racists, and Nazis, do we? I mean the idea that we all have inner somethings or others that are deep seated, unchangeable, intractable, inevitable, and true, of which our bodies are the outward sign?

Sentences are word games, so we can play with them. A gender riff might help discern what's heinous about the language in the seemingly generous sentence at hand: "L.'s handsomeness, in the midst of chemotherapy, exemplifies his true inner strength." It doesn't quite work on so many levels. In fact, it's nonsensical and ludicrous.

"L.'s being the strong, quiet type, in the midst of chemotherapy, exemplifies his true inner muscle bulge."

"L.'s erectness, in the midst of chemotherapy, exemplifies his true inner manliness."

"L.'s hunkiness, in the midst of chemotherapy, exemplifies his true inner fuck-all attitude."

It just doesn't translate, and the more I repeat it, I notice the grammatical lapse in the use of the commas: isn't "in the midst of chemotherapy" an essential phrase?

I can't really think of a *trait* a man could be expected to *preserve* on chemotherapy, which tells me that men continue to enjoy the genderless status of humans where women are bound to their bodies as females and girls. Our cancer subject, L., the sentence says, remained a woman on chemotherapy; her femininity wasn't effaced. That's the main thing. And that's what matters.

I never felt the loss of the "feminine" in chemotherapy—would that such a liberation were possible! But I did feel acutely, at a certain far along point, that I was beginning to become something other than human. By the end, there's no question that one feels like a horse driven in circles inside a ring. Jean and I together attempt the impossible at this time—*to disrupt a ritual*—in an effort to help me to feel differently and better. We give me oats. We brush me down. We race. If we trotted inside the paddock last week, this week we run our hands across the embellishments that dress my bridle before a treatment session begins.

The feeling is that something you relied on, however imaginary, is beginning to "break," and it's not one's actual body that is being ground down (though obviously that is happening, too) but some unseen mechanism that daily props it up—the so-called spirit. At a point of increased submission to the difficult routine, I write to a friend: "I'm beginning to feel like what they do to horses and falcons," but the more I think about it, I realize that humans have invented such a varied assortment of techniques of submission (including our current penchant for torture) that the analogy to breaking a wild horse or taming a falcon is not exactly perfect.

Birds wear bells on their legs and identity bands (that seems right). The falconer wears a gauntlet for self-protection (see the nurse's special outerwear). The bird is held captive (the first time you walk to the bathroom tethered to your chemo IV and see the urine turned pink by Adriamycin, a sense of captivity sets in). It's not the romance you were hoping for this year. The bird hunts for his trainer because he begins to become reliant on him as a predictable food source. The trainer doesn't need the bird to secure his own survival—he trains him for "sport." Here's where the analogy stops working because, of course, the aim of my paces and the captors who keep calling me back isn't to assure them of their dominance or make me forever dependent on their care but to free me of the disease that has overtaken me.

Is it really, anyway, my spirit that is broken, or a *style* that I've come to rely on, a style of radical will? It's true that I feel as though my spirit is beginning to break, but I'm suspicious, and for good reason, of the very concept of spirit, not least because of the way it confers clairvoyance, or x-ray vision, on others. It's astounding to me how, in particular, *strangers* become prophets, oracles, soothsayers at this time, readers of my inner self, gaugers of my spirit. A clerk in a wig shop sizes my character up and concludes, eye to eye, with utter confidence, "*You*'re going to be ok." I feel sorry for those who she can tell will not be. An herbalist in a tea shop draws a frame around my face with the thumb and index finger of each hand, as though sizing me up for a photograph of my true self. She shakes her head, "No." This is all in a day's easy work. "*You*'re not going to die of cancer. You don't have the death aura." My goodness! What does one tell a person who *does*?

My attitude and my sense of humor also seem indicative of future good fortune. Because I say that I'm praying to Our Lady of Perpetual Queasiness. Because when asked, "How are you?" I say, "Today I've managed to tamp down my suicidal ideation." But these presumed indicators of spirit really won't divert the course of my cancer or assure my outliving it even if, in my heart of hearts, I'd very much prefer to die of something else. Health insurance and other material guarantors are more reliable in this regard, including the material resource that makes possible the sudden appearance of healing hands—of massage therapists, hairdressers, acupuncturists, and physical therapists—on the many days my horse-broken body needs to be brushed down.

One day my friend, Jim, asks me to tell him what I do in the course of a day; another time, he asks me what I'm reading. "These are questions to ask a normal person," I growl through the telephone, "and I'm not currently normal!" It's hard to explain how time is eaten when you need to swish with a baking soda and salt water solution before and after each attempt at a meal. Or the work involved in downing two quarts of water in a day even if you're nauseated, or the energy required to fend off the raw agony of mouth sores. That you should follow a hot shower with a cold, according to my European friends, and take special care thoroughly to clean yourself before and after each visit to the bathroom because, as you've been reminded, A/C destroys the entire lining of the alimentary tract, "beginning at the tip of the tongue and ending at the anus." Between that matter-of-fact instruction and the destruction of white blood cells, any orifice is ripe as a site for infection. One of my greatest fears is the development of a particularly nasty-sounding side effect from the list: hemorrhagic cystitis. I walk home in terror when my ophthalmologist instructs, after examining my exfoliating eyes, "Give me a call if they start to bleed." Halloween was just around the corner. Worse than any of these horror shows combined, though, was the idea of the effects of a broken spirit.

The shadow of the cousin who, soon after her child died, up and died herself. "They said she died of a broken heart." The rictus of the broken man. The need to turn away from life *in order to live* while you are inserted into a mechanics of elemental survival: rise;

if possible, eat; swish; piss, clean yourself thereafter; drowse; eat, if possible; swish; drink; piss.

I know what I don't want to lose in the face of what breast cancer treatment demands of me in the twenty-first century, what I don't wish to forfeit, efface, erode, and it's not my femininity, or my beauty, inner or outer; it's not my inner strength (I've always been a big believer in the power of admitting to weakness). More than ever, what I pray against all odds to maintain, is my capacity both to *love* and to be *in love*.

To lose the object of our desire: this is something most of us experience repeatedly in the course of a lifetime. When we succeed in coping with such a loss, Freud calls it "mourning"; when we refuse, he calls it "melancholia." To lose, on the other hand, the desire to desire is something altogether greater and possibly irreparable. Certainly a little temporary hell, like chemotherapy, cannot destroy a person's desire to desire, can it? No link has been discovered between bone marrow depletion and desire, I don't think. If *to love* is to treat others with the utmost ethical regard, to be *in love* is to cultivate the capacity to play together, to keep alive each other's desire. To be in love is to take the risk of imagining with others. To wait, even to have the ability to wait.

Gillian Rose's *Love's Work*, the philosopher's tour de force to emerge from the ovarian cancer that caused her death, opens with an epigraph from Staretz Silouan: "Keep your mind in hell, and despair not." I'm suggesting a simple revision: "Stay in love in hell and despair not." "Remain in the hell of being in love and despair not." This particular "in love" of which I speak is one that begins at a point of catastrophe rather than as a defense against it. On chemotherapy, I want to translate everything that is written to me into a language other than English, and in this way, transform the most banal utterance into a declaration of love so that I can pine, long for, and imagine being wanted. It's the privilege of being at loggerheads that I miss on chemotherapy; it's the enchantment of being en rapport.

Feelings. Wo wo wo. Feelings. Chemotherapy offers the opportunity of an anatomy of tears. Can you make yourself cry? Will crying restore your humanity?

The conditions that produce tears in us, the situations that bring us to tears, are culturally determined and oddly individuating all at once. I cry at what I've come to call "'Hey, Buddy,' moments." It's a personal mythology laced with ideological fervor. A motorist asks an officer of the law, "Hey, Buddy, can I make a left?" and the uniformed man's reply fills me with tears! It's a sort of reliance on the kindness of strangers sentimentality that overtakes me, apparently stripped of rhyme or reason. It's bizarre. Jean rarely cries, or at least doesn't melt as easily as I, but her eyes well up to flooding when she witnesses a formally consummate work of art, especially if, in the form of music, beauty and dissonance coalesce. Old *Lassie* episodes also produce a glint.

On chemo, bodies produce newly calibrated types of tears. We're preparing a meal, and something that I say about the way I'm feeling makes me start to cry, and before I know it, Jean is crying too, and we're just all water across the table from one another without hugging yet, we cry and cry. "It's all we've been through catching up with us," I say, and I can't remember too many times in our twentysome years together that we've cried in synch like this because it usually seems better if one person consoles while the other person cries, it's scary if both members of the family cry uncontrollably like this, it must mean that something has been let loose or is falling apart, but it feels to me like reckless lovemaking and simultaneous orgasm, this mutuality of tears, and when it's over it feels as though these were detoxifying tears, the poisons literally exiting the body in endless streams.

Then there are the "for your eyes only" tears when the grief crowds you, and you cover yourself in it as if to replace a shroud with a blanket, as if to be pelted with petals of lamentation indifferent to the cat's playfulness or the fact of something warming that you're simmering on the stove. The cat bats at a red ribbon and prances which only makes the feeling worse. There is no aroma. All scents are crowded out by a knife-blade cry because, if you can laugh at yourself, which is a good habit to cultivate, you should also be able to grieve for yourself—on this particularly fine day, tears prompted by the realization that you probably aren't going to have the chance to live a long life. To see old age, and older. To make and to ripen. "She had both breasts cut off, my aunt!" Mike the Italian tailor demonstrates. "Phht, Phht," he slashes across both sides of his chest, "and that was thirty years ago and now she's ninety, no more problem!" "Really?" I say, "Wow!" But I don't believe that this could be true for me.

Finally, the strangest tears of all are those perversely anti-endorphin ones I shed while exercising. I can't ever recall having experienced this before. It usually comes on just when I begin to feel my heart pumping, and because the breathing is already strained from running in place, the cry comes out as a *eyeah eyeah eyeah* sound preceded by a blustery whimper. Exercising and crying seem inimical in the way that dancing and crying might. It seems like something the body should not be able to do.

Before chemo began, I was determined to purchase an elliptical trainer. I'd been warned that gyms were out of the question because of their open-to-the-public germs, and I'd read that daily exercise, if it were at all possible, could help both to cope with chemo and to hasten recovery. It was a "take charge" urge that found the machine, it was an "I'm gonna beat this" impulse that sent me in search of this headless two-armed bandit that was meant to save me. The unwieldy, immovable thing, purchased on Craigslist for four hundred dollars less than list price and paid for by my father (the only thing he's ever given me, the only thing I've ever asked for), had to be wedged through our bulkhead and into the basement by four of my most strapping friends who also succeeded in dismantling parts of it without instructions. Something about this purchase felt insane.

Ever the considerate one, knowing that sound travels easily from the basement, I play opera rather than Earth, Wind & Fire when I know our tenant is in the house, never considering that she might hate opera. I'm crying. Not because the final aria of *La Traviata* was also the last thing my grandfather taught me to play on the mandolin, because in point of fact I'm perfectly capable of surrendering my lips to Maria Callas' lips, her voice to my ear, and there's nothing sad to me about this. I'm crying because I recognize where I am. I'm on a treadmill of trying (even though the machine is called an elliptical trainer). Once again, I'm being asked to prove myself in the final heat. I'm crying because trying is trying; because I'm all about effort and effort is compensatory. When life requires extra laps from me, my running joke is that I was born on a Saturday, and Saturday's child must "work for a living." "You look like you're gathering okra," my Tai Chi instructor, a supremely serene pony-tailed Irishman offered as he stood at a nonjudgmental distance, bemused by my effort to master a practice that was all about ease. Trying too hard is laced with pathos, whether it's something you have to do or something you tend to do. The overly effortful jog is an emblem for so many other extra efforts, which must be a sign of the need to please some Other whose love is too painfully unreliable, too precarious, and for whose sake you give everything you have away.

Jean and I lived for part of the year 2002 in Rome. I worked very hard, *of course*, to get a research leave and got one. At a certain splendid juncture in our time there, my mother came to visit with her friend, Eileen. Together we explored the town my mother's father came from, Teano, and nearby Naples: "You look like a Neapolitan," her grandmother had always told her, so we went to find out if that was true. We wandered quietly in the Church of Gesu Nuovo while, in one part of the church, people were having their confessions heard, while in another part of the church, a wedding ceremony was underway. We marveled as much at the architecture as at the tinseled walls, walls covered from floor to ceiling with ex votos in silver that people had hung, each one indicative of an ailment in need of curing. We bought a supply of our own—I remember treating the matter metaphorically, and making my donation toward a silver-plated model of a pair of eyes. I wanted to see better, more clearly, further, so I chose the eyes. "Americans seem to have a lot of problems," the man at the counter remarked (all of this was inside the massive edifice that is the church) as we presented him with our donation and supply. "Yes, we have a lot of problems," I said, and realized what was worse: we wouldn't be hanging these in a church, or using them as they were intended, but adding them to the accoutrements that made our domiciles properly bourgeois.

Just prior to our purchase of some ex votos, Eileen and I had found ourselves inside a room inside the church: a transposition of the entire consulting room of a man they called "the saintly doctor," including the armchair in which he died: "Prof. Joseph Moscati, A True Christian Doctor...while visiting some patients at his private consulting room, he suddenly felt unwell. He gently dismissed all, sat in his armchair, and quietly, without agony, gave up his soul to God." A priest apparently saw us exiting the consulting-room-homage and now asked all four of us—Jean, my mother, Eileen and me—if we wished to receive his benediction, a blessing he would give using a relic of Saint Joseph Moscati, a chip off one of the old guy's bones. A blessing isn't the sort of thing one refuses, Catholic or lapsed, and so we accepted, and he began, waving the relic across our bodies, touching us each on our foreheads and reciting a special prayer.

Just afterwards, I heard him chatting with the man who sold the icons. I understood him asking, "Who *is* this woman?" and pointing to me. But I didn't entirely understand the rest. The clerk translated: "The priest wants to know who you are."

"Yes, I got that part," I said.

"I told him you're an American visiting Naples."

"*Si, capisco.*" (I got that part too.)

"He says you're special." That part I didn't get. "That you have a very pure heart. He says, you're unusually *devout.*"

I learned long ago never to trust the compliments of a priest—

the church is a business in the end, even an empire in search of souls to colonize, and capital. Given the fact that I'm thoroughly irreligious, the priest's reading of my inner self as devout became our joke for the day. "He's right," I said to my friends and family, to my lover, as we left, "I am devout. He just doesn't know *who* or *what* I'm devoted *to*."

Never deny me my devotion. To pleasure, to art, to social justice, to. . . . Let me be faithful, obedient, and passionate to you and towards you. It's possible obedience and passion aren't mutually exclusive: today a horse, tomorrow a falcon. Greatest fear: that I will fall out of love with . . . (see, libidinal link). Libidinal link: see artist Miriam Engelberg's comic strip, the work she devoted herself to even after her breast cancer metastasized in under three years and with no warning, no expectation, to her brain. Greatest fear: that I will fall out of love with you, dear reader, or you with me. Fondest memory (libidinal link): my mother's poetry, the rhythms of which rocked me in my cradle, from cradle to grave and chemotherapy in-between. My mother's poetry that went:

Shall I Tell You How I Spend My Day

Blackbirds bite me awake
From dreams of death

I start to work
Catching apples that
Roll from the
Painting on the wall

I'm hungry but
These apples are too live to eat
Mischievous fruit
Make me chase them

I can't stop laughing
Neither can Cezanne

Outside
People exhaust the air

I must neglect these apples
If I'm to accomplish anything

Water draws me
Where the creek
Runs through the city's core
It drowns out human hammerings
With the sound of its cool
Cauldron boil

Trees slide down its banks
Red mites run on my white page
Afraid of the afternoon moon

An artist misses
A tree
Heavy with dripping cankerberries

An alarm reminds me
I must forget who I am
If I'm to
Remember who I am

I return to sleep

· 4 ·

Radiation:

story

"The science of radiography is based on the fact that X-rays can penetrate through an object, whereas visible light cannot."

—*The Stereofloral Radiography of Albert G. Richards,* Museum of Jurassic Technology, Los Angeles

"Nice To Know: Receiving external radiation treatments is just like having an X-ray taken. The procedure is painless, and you will not hear, see, or smell the radiation."

—www.ehealthmd.com

there's an inside and an outside to radiation. There are rooms within rooms, and each one takes on the cast of a complex sociology because what happens in the "sim" room is different from what happens in the treatment room, which is different from what transpires in the locker room in which you daily change from street clothes into hospital gown and back again, which is separate from the waiting room where genders mingle and types of cancer too, and these rooms are joined by corridors, lined, if you take the wrong way in, by the hospital's plumbing system and low-lying ducts snaking their industrial way like guideposts in a subterranean matrix, but if you enter the right way, are lined with fishless aquariums, brightly lit and colorful but devoid of fish because there was something wrong with the filtering system of these tanks so all the fish died.

Perhaps the most pressing motivation for regaining the full range of motion in my surgical arm was something my physical therapist had said: she told me that I would be expected to hold my arm above my head for a long period of time, anywhere from a half hour to an hour, for the initial session during which a simulation of the radiation treatment field is composed. "If you can't hold your arm above your head, they have to tie it in place."

How would you picture such a tie? I didn't imagine leather restraints or rubber hoses. To my mind's eye, the tie that might have to hold my too-weak arm in place if I failed to recover in time is a ripped and tattered piece of cloth, the kind that pirates tear out of their victim's sweat-drenched clothing with a swipe of their swords. A sort of expediency. Racks came to mind, and bowels of ships, but that might have been because I also knew the "sim" session would entail tattooing.

Radiation is to oncology as dermatology and podiatry are to the rest of medical science. Such hierarchies are silly and inaccurate at their core, and yet it was hard not to wonder what drove the decision to house the Radiation Oncology Department in the Cancer Center's basement. It only lent more fervor to the image of radiation involving something diabolical, Frankensteinian, the mixing of alloys, the testing of outer limits, men in lab coats measuring invisible rays. It was equipped with doors many layers thick, thicker even than the opening to a precious vault or a medieval castle. Its basement setting must be a sign of the hospital's collective unconscious remembering that fallout shelters sported radioactive logos and were generally underground. The reversal was a form of forgetting: we are *so* safe in this great country of ours that now we go underground to *receive* radiation.

A cross between a laboratory and an industrial bakery (I swore I smelled rising dough), the prospect of radiation once I had arrived there filled me with more dread than any of my former, presumably more caustic, more invasive forms of treatment, even though the radiation oncology personnel were uniformly kind.

Perhaps it was the girth of the machine's looming that alarmed me. "La Machine!," I kept hearing in my head, but wasn't that an ad for a yogurt maker or tiny French car? Perhaps it was the distance in the sim room between the many-inches-thick door and the steel berth upon which my plotters left me, at least half a football field away. An entire *team* appeared to set my sim in place—their intensity impressed me: the concentration with which they guided their spacecraft above and around me; the exactitude with which they positioned their hovering devices; the looks on their faces that showed them fastened to something glorious in the beyond; the care with which they adjusted my arm in its overhead cradle; the panache with which they tattooed my breast; their attitude of maniacal pleasure toward the machine's ability—in concert with their manicured movements, their positioning the body to a tee, their baby-sized rulers—to deliver on target as they fled the room and left me to dangle in outer space.

Thank goodness this is a public hospital so I don't have to be greeted by religious icons in the department's halls, and yet a telling word blazed in red is, daily, the first thing to meet my eye: FAITH, a poster implores, each letter hewn like a row of unlit matches above a primitive rendering of a pair of dangling socks. The representation showed a degree of craftsmanship nearing the pinnacle of my grade school fire prevention posters. A bit out of the loop, and loopy too, how was I to know this was the official logo of the Boston Red Sox?

My oncologist radiologist—or was it the other way around, my radiation oncologist?— my doctor, wears a bow tie. He more nearly resembles Caruso than I, his face cherubic and Renaissance Italian. He has the features of an altar boy and the annoying habit of helping me down from the examining table: it's not that high from the floor, and I'm not exactly a lady-in-waiting, but he every time takes my hand in his and then my elbow the better to prevent my dainty foot from being soiled outside the carriage door. Need I mention that the examination involves his feeling my breast with a doughy paw? The bow tie says, "used car salesman," but the face says, "angel, chapel, last rites, extreme unction, Mamma's boy." He has a scuffed larynx, I conclude from the scratchy sound of his voice, damaged no doubt by radiation scatter, chafed by yelling out car prices at auction, by scolding his kids, strained by singing.

"I know this isn't your domain, it's left over from chemo-therapy, but my main complaint right now is that my mouth is not improving," I tell him in one of our weekly sessions. "Are you brushing your tongue?" he asks. "Yes," I reply, figuring he's playing the straight man to the name of my current condition—hairy tongue—"since I have no hair on my head to brush, I brush my tongue daily." His two female colleagues enjoy my joke with me. He closes his lips tightly and thinks. "Maybe your whole head is having trouble recovering," he says. Is this a veiled slight to my cleverness? No. He means by my "head," a brainless entity; he means, as he puts it, that my hair also seems to be coming back rather slowly; ergo, my mouth cells are slow to return as well.

"Will this treatment affect the sensation in my breast?" I had asked the intern early on. "Will it diminish sexual sensation?" She looked at me as though this question had never appeared on the exam, at which point I couldn't fail to notice that the sleeve of her white lab coat was black. With no sleep at her disposal and a generalized dishevelment that she tried to keep at bay, sensation of any variety was the last thing on her mind.

"And on the roof sat the judge." My brothers and I would be both frightened and tickled by this line pronounced ominously, with guttural glee, by Danny Kaye on our $33\frac{1}{3}$ rpm record of *Grimm's Fairy Tales* as performed by the master. The tale was about a band of animal musicians who overtake a cottage filled with thieves, one of whom is so frightened by the animals, he hallucinates the dog as a man with a knife, the cat as a witch, the donkey as a monster, and the cock as a judge who cries, "Bring the rogue here to me!" "And on the roof sat the judge" was how I came to think of the radiation goose, a large plastic figure perched in the reception area who overheard me every morning recite my date of birth and who wore different "outfits" depending upon the impending holiday. "Where were his outfits manufactured?" I wondered. With great curiosity, I considered, "His caps and jackets, his scarves and his vests—where were they stowed?"

"Radiation" in the abstract equals a single episode in most people's minds and it doesn't, from the outside, appear to bear the onus of chemotherapy. But the thick and thin of it amounts, in most breast cancer cases, to thirty-five sessions, every day, five days a week, for seven weeks. In the course of any treatment, several holidays are sure to come and go. Seasons may even change, which meant in my treatment scenario, the sudden transformation of the framed prints that hung in the corridors and waiting rooms into Christmas packages. I'd never seen this act performed upon a wall hanging before—to trap a painting top to bottom, left to right, in bright red cellophane and affix a golden bow. Gift packaging isn't a very interesting thing to hang on a wall. We might have liked the paintings, we might have preferred them, but we had to give ourselves over as we walked from waiting room to radiation room to a decking of the halls.

"Will it affect sensation?" I had asked the intern, and she really couldn't say, or at least failed to provide me with an answer, but I notice acutely, and maybe because of the "invisible" nature of radiation treatment, sights, scents, and sounds. I didn't know, for example, that teeth would be involved in my treatment, but as I lie on the table, a small window attached to one of the machine's large arms comes into view and inside this window a set of jaws that clamps into place. Long teeth appear from above and below inside the window like pistons or drill bits. The teeth don't meet but form a misshaped mouth, an eye, really, as I come to understand that the space between them equals the shape of the area they will radiate on my body, and the teeth are leaves, made of lead, called multileaf collimators—they block out one area in order to highlight another.

I look into this window and it looks into me and I hear music: if I had perfect pitch, I could tell you the tone that meets an ear for the length of time the radiation penetrates: B-flat? C-sharp? Sound accompanies the body in place of sight. "What form does the radiation take?" I ask one of my radiologists, a man with the unbelievable name of Sneezy. "How does it not disperse into air like a cloud and miss me?" I ask. "The machine acts like a gun," he says, "and the radiation is like a bullet." He has a Texas drawl and a moustache that I'm certain had taken the shape of a handlebar in his youth but that now hangs down like walrus tufts on either side. "That's my breast!" I say to Sneezy, surprised to see my body part as shadow puppet in the long arm's window. "You'd know that breast anywhere, wouldn't you?" Sneezy reminds me of W. C. Fields, of Mae West, he plays his words on his tongue like a bow to a violin string. "Stay nice n' still fer me now. Heeeere we go." And he flees the room. B-flat. C-sharp. Red light flashing. Rays like bullets enter my cells at the level of their DNA. Demolition work. Burning. While through the radiation room's loudspeakers today, tomorrow, "Let It Snow, Let it Snow, Let it Snow" and "Jingle Bell, Jingle Bell, Jingle Bell Rock."

Let me not be mistaken. Let me not forsake my senses. Sneezy smells like alcohol—should I report him?—because a person couldn't drink and carry out this exacting work, not even if they were a "functioning alcoholic." On second sniff, I realize I'm terribly wrong: it's not whiskey that Sneezy reeks of but an alcohol-based aftershave. But one of the other women in the locker room smells most definitely of a drink too many now seeping through her pores, and cigarettes, too. Don't ask me what it means that the doctor smells like ammonia and another radiologist, as early as 8:00 a.m., smells of peanut butter. He doesn't appear to be eating anything, but the peanut butter smell is unmistakable. And consistent. He never *doesn't* smell of peanut butter. Is there such a thing as peanut butter chewing gum? Each morning when I dress and undress for the second time, lifting my shirt up over my head, I notice I smell of nearly ripened strawberries, of apricots, of blood oranges, and sage. Of aloe vera gel, of the desert, of mineral oil, of last night's antiradiation lentils, of hot flash sweat.

Radiation is odorless and invisible, which to a lay consciousness might suggest that it is dead, inert, but death has an odor too, and a visibility even if we would prefer not to see it. Radiation is a dead-not-dead-but-deadly substance. Its evidence over time in the burns that appear on your skin proves it is invasive even if invisible. Of course, most of what constitutes life on earth, the atmosphere we breathe, the bodies we live in, the shape of our thoughts, the force of gravity, the shift from night to day, and all else we have no names for, is beyond the scope of our sight. Scientists try to bring things into view with instruments; writers, with words, each reckoning in their way with the limits of human perception, which doesn't even begin to account for what we fail to see for lack of looking, or what we cannot hear because of the ideological contours of our particular day, convention's brand and say.

I do have a sense that I must focus my attention if I'm to survive my treatment journey. On what, you might ask? *Focus away*, I could answer, from the fact that the current moment is full of amputees and that this *whole thing* could blow up in my face. You might think a hauntedness would pervade the place where they administer radiation given the daily application of a treatment substance *we cannot see*. How unnerving is *that*? But they can and do see this stuff—the doctors and technicians put their trust in math to determine the ray's intensity and path, its depth of penetration and dose, the angle of its administration and flight—and their calculations had better be rock solid. I, meanwhile, live in a world of trying to pay attention and missing so much as a result, of heeding and still not seeing, of noticing and imprinting, of glimpsing and forgetting, of sensing and dwelling, of turning my senses, my filaments, my skin, my fur, to the wall of science for a time, for a spell.

I've walked into and out of the same treatment room daily, barring weekends, but not until day twenty-three do I notice a mural four feet high and ten feet wide that takes up most of a wall. The mural is large enough to approximate a panorama. It's of ocean waves, blue-grey and white, beating against rocks. Lying on the treatment table, I notice that the mural, no doubt hung with the idea of calming the patients, is too low to see from where I'm perched. "You know, you can't really see that mural from here," I tell my therapists. "We know," they say. "It used to light up, but one day it just stopped working." (see fish tanks) Still, I'm temporarily flummoxed by the thought that I could walk into and out of the room twenty-three times and never notice the mural. What had I been looking at, and what was different about today that I noticed it now? "When you notice the mural on the treatment wall, it will be time for you to leave." I imagined the sighting as a mystical kung fu test, but I still had twelve sessions left to go.

One day I notice a pile of awkward sculptures stacked every which way on a cart. Lava-like forms, abstract shapes hollowed out in asymmetric patterns mounted onto glass. I ask my peanut butter-scented therapist about them, and he explains that each one is the design of a treatment path for a particular person. These odd puzzle shapes, as I understand it, are used in an older machine, the machine without the movable teeth, and the figuration is both the area to be targeted and the area to be blocked. "Feel how heavy they are," he hands me one, and I practically re-injure my "surgical arm." I want to know what they're made of, I want to be their student. I note and proudly recite by rote: "cadmium, bismuth, tin, and lead." I don't know why I expect to learn in a day what my radiologists took years to master, but there's a yen to understand the nature of the treatment beast that acts upon me, the material makeup of the system I'm being inserted into, the sphere of influence I'm being made to enter, its particles meeting my particulars and vice versa.

I intuit a physics made of vectors of desire, from my childhood rock collection to my prepubescent dream—and wasn't it every girl's dream?—of becoming an archaeologist, to my first encounter with the excavations of Sigmund Freud, to a professor named Sussman twisting an imaginary ball of twine between his hands as he explained to us that the psychoanalytic psyche was structured like an onion, to this moment of my sedimented body prone on a steel table penetrated by manufactured rays, dominoes unstuck from the periodic tables I once memorized, blocked by an amalgam of metals. Curiosity isn't doused by my disease but re-ignited in this space between flesh, and bone, and bismuth.

I think when my doctor looks at me he sees a field. A plain. I think he sees a series of plains. A set of fields. Just as when I look at him I see an altar boy. One day, very far along in my treatment regimen, I see for the first time myself. Myself as the treatment pictures me. My head is cocked to the left—this is my treatment position—my right arm is in its cradle, my butt is flush against the "butt-stop," when I see for the first time, reflected in the glass of the box that hovers above me and to one side, my dossier. I see my photograph on a computer screen outside the room but looking in at me, a smiling head shot of a person with hair, I see but can't read all manner of data. Fade in, fade out, bleed in, bleed out, like the disappearing fresco in Fellini's *Roma*, the entire screen, photo and all, is replaced by another dossier. In the place where my face had been appears an image of the "field," which appears both to fill up and close up to the tune of B-flat. C-sharp.

But none of these sightings, like moments of unanticipated truth, like calls from within the wilds of science to the senses to see or hear or smell, like "stations" in a ritual in transfigured time, had the staying power of the first things ever to meet my eye. Lying, head to one side, you have no choice in the matter of what portion of the visible world you'll be made to gaze at, nor for how long. What I saw in my first and all subsequent treatment sessions were cubbyholes filled, each to its own, with hats. The hats were made of stiff, white webbing and shaped like the helmets that British bobbies wear, tall and narrow, and some appeared to have initials taped to their fronts. "What's with the pith helmets?" I jumped off the table, my first treatment out of thirty-five down.

"We engage in fencing tournaments at the end of each day," my peanutty therapist replied and mock lunged. "No," he looked at me, not at them, "those are for radiating the head. They hold the person's head in place and block parts we don't want to radiate."

"Stay nice and still for me now. Here we go!" Unable to turn away, and not willing to shut my eyes for fear of falling, every day I gaze toward macabre cubbyholes filled with sinister hats. I count the rows, I try to make out initials, like fingering the letters on a grave, I try to imagine faces, standing, walking, lying figures to whom the hats belong. But even though I'm here beside them, and know they're there, my senses don't allow me to fill the hats with heads.

~———◠

If we return enough to a particular place, we call that place a haunt, or a hang-out, the square walls of a comforting atmosphere, sometimes a meeting place but also possibly a portal of aloneness, sought after. There are places we choose to return to together—the diner where my writing partner and I met nearly weekly for a year—and places that put us in close proximity to each other without our ever meeting—the daily trip on the bus or subway. There are places, less determinate, more mercurial, but for all their abstractness, still convincing, points in time or circumstance, stirrings of unnamed desire where our *lives cross over.* We refer to a "meeting of minds" which we might even be able to have without actually meeting; in fact, meeting "in person" is known to ruin many an intimate e-mail correspondence. I like to picture my closest meetings with others as a cross-hatch—for the way, in painting, the term allows for shadow and volume; for the way, in language, it admits of something being born. But some people feel better met by nonhumans than by other people, and some, reclusive, by an obsession all their own, unshareable, but better company than they can find in peers. "I just don't know how to *meet* people." "You need to meet *more* people." "I need to meet *new* people." "Have we *met?*" "I wish we'd *never met!*"

There must be a relationship between the form and extent of our meetings with others and our individual reckoning with an essential solitude, the kind that many people feel most acutely in illness as a forebear of that profounder moment of total leave-taking that each of us makes alone. I begin to wonder if some men are drawn to soldiering because they believe that battlefields are places where they won't die solo. Emily Dickinson writes solitudes: of "space," of "sea," of "Death," and of the "soul admitted to itself," which she calls a "polar privacy." I find there's nothing more alone-making than the fact of my radiologists' flat white backs, the snow-swept tundra, the tabula rasa of no return, of the backs of their lab coats as they exit the treatment room, because even if *the many* in the course of a day are subjected to radiation's beams, these rays that might heal you or might harm you or both and neither—they simply might fail to stop a cancer in its course—for those moments, even if the technician insists, "We're right outside!," *you* are the only person being treated; you are truly alone if only because you are being done to and they are doing, and the danger of being done to requires that they leave while you stay put and watch while they move on and out, leaving you with the undecoded canvas of their flat white backs.

All of the love and support in the world cannot and perhaps should not cancel out the fundamental aloneness one experiences at various points in the course of a treatment for cancer. This being forced back on oneself and the sense that one is where others *are not* impresses some people with a melancholic sense of isolation, while it turns others in the direction of a belief in God. For my own part, I hope I get to live long enough to see whether my being forced to know aloneness so acutely will, with time, enable me to be, when I'm with people, more profoundly there, better able to *meet* them wherever they are, even if I'm not sure exactly what that means.

Alongside the cold invisibility of the treatment method, and the floes of polar aloneness from which you wave at passing tundra, *being with others* turns out to be the surprise feature of radiation. It's another of many treatment details that no one told you to expect. To arrive at radiation is to arrive at narrative; radiation therapy has a social aspect that is felicitous, at least for a day. Seeing many of the same people in the waiting room for such an extended period of days encourages conversation, and yet there are other forces in a cancer ward that compel people to share, to blurt, to confide, or to confess, and a great deal can be learned in just one encounter about one's fellow journeyers, even if you never see each other again.

It only takes a minute in the locker room for me to learn that this is another woman's second time here. We're both sighing over how tiring the daily trek is when she tells me she had cervical cancer for which she was treated eight months ago, but the cancer has recurred in a place they say they've never seen cancer before. I don't ask her to specify. She tells me she had internal radiation which required a hospital stay and that it was one of the worst experiences of her life. She hopes I can avoid it. Another woman's half-hung gown reveals a deep red well where a port might have been. "Oh, it was terrible!" she draws close. "My body rejected the port. I had all sorts of infections. They had to remove the port, so now I have a pick!" She points to an area under her arm, but I don't edge closer to get a better view. I've never heard of a pick, and I picture her chemo needing to be administered with a pickax. I take my place in the waiting room next to a woman who is a cross between Rosalind Russell and my mother's sister, Bea, but maybe this is because Russell once played the part of a beautiful nun, a role my aunt played in real life, and the woman next to me wears her wig like a wimple on a broad-chested torso atop a high cheek-boned, arched eyebrowed face. She has two kinds of cancer, or possibly three, bilaterally (in both breasts). Her entire upper chest above her gown line looks sunburnt. She's confused, she says, it's so confusing. The question of whether her breast cancers are positive in one way, or negative in another, and she leafs through a pile of concerns that include possible sarcoma in one breast, blood clots in her lungs caused by Irimidex, and her sister's breast cancer that has metastasized to her bones. "I don't know why God doesn't spare me," she says. "I've lived my life." She's sixty-two-years old. A red-haired, middle-aged man tells me this is his third time here. He gets cancer every other year but only on the even years. "First I had breast cancer," he explains, "then prostate, and now I have it in my back." A misread chest X-ray led his brother to an untimely cancer death, but their father lived for twenty years with cancer. The second time I see this man he begins to tell me everything again. He seems to recognize me but stares straight ahead as he recounts his story afresh and from the start. "Yes," I say, ending the story for him as he had the day before, "but your father lived with cancer for twenty years," as if my reminding him that I know his story could negate his need for renarration. Sometimes our scripts seem composed by Harold Pinter, punctuated as they are by pregnant pauses and a back and forth that really isn't cognizant of two; other times, I think it's Beckett we're performing, as when this man addresses not me but a never-present Godot.

One man dealing with colon and lung cancer has suffered the dislodging of his port. His wife, her eyes ringed with dark circles, speeds past the waiting room en route to an appointment. "How's John doing?" I ask.

"They had to go in through the groin!"

"What a nightmare!" I yell back. Let us recall that the port is located in the chest.

It only takes a few days of hearing people's stories to realize I'm exhausted. Radiation causes fatigue, we're told, though they're not entirely sure of the mechanisms that bring it on. It's possible the immune system begins to head full force in the direction of the part of the body being bombarded, but degrees of tiredness remain variable and hard to predict even if a great number of breast cancer patients say they "hit a brick wall" around weeks three or four. Clearly, it's the social aspect that is most draining; what Miriam

Engelberg calls "compassion fatigue." Which is perhaps why we distance ourselves from each other in waiting rooms by determining each other's "type." Each of us has a custom-made "mold" in radiation, and each of us cuts a type of a figure. I don't know what sort of a telltale mark my fellow patients knew me by or as, but I recognized each of them in easily identifying ways as if to better place them, just as each of us took nearly precisely the same chair in the same part of the waiting room each day, like family members at a table, or kids who know their place in school. There was he of the weak salute, and she who was, no question, the nicest person you'd ever want to meet. There was the dashing, gallant man who accompanied his perfectly coifed and nervous sister-in-law; there was the determined Spanish-speaking woman who didn't wear a wig, and there was a woman I came to call, as if returned to elementary school, "blabber mouth" (but only to myself and Jean).

If, at first, the sense of community that radiation offers brings delight to a beleaguered cancer patient, in no time at all, the community splits into cliques and even occasionally brings us all back to adolescent dynamics we thought we'd never want to return to, or had, at least quite long ago, "survived." I wondered if it was the fact of having lockers that led one woman to begin whispering into the ear of another woman: was she inviting her to a party without inviting us all? I try not to return in my mind to the torture and conflict of the person I was the last time I had a locker. I try not to remember punching my locker over the demands of an overbearing woman teacher who inappropriately sought the "attentions" of my adolescent self. I try not to return to weird moments at my locker on those occasions on which the homecoming queen would ask me to inspect her ass as she walked away so as to assure her that her menstrual pad wasn't visible through her pants. "Let me know if you can see anything, Mare," and I was made to turn my gaze toward her bouncingly vigorous butt without desiring her. She was both the captain of the lacrosse team and the head of the cheerleading squad, who pounded their words into opponents and home team alike by spelling them: "And we're BIG, B-I-G, and we're BAD, B-A-D, and we're BOSS, B-O-S-S, B-O-S-S BOSS," followed by "BE AGGRESSIVE, BE AGGRESSSIVE, B-E A-G-G-R-E-S-S-I-V-E."

How vivid were the hierarchies: a clear-cut difference between the "seniors" who were almost finished with radiation treatment and who enjoyed a camaraderie in one part of the room, and the "freshmen" who were just starting out who shifted awkwardly in their chairs in another part of the room. Blabber mouth was a senior when I was a freshman, and though we sat in distant parts of the waiting area, I tried to bridge the gap by one day sharing notes on how we might decide whether to participate in a clinical trial, or not, that would require monthly trips for several years to the hospital for intravenous administration of a drug with a list of side effects as long as those of chemo. If you won the lottery and got to take the drug by mouth, you'd have to be sure to sit up straight for a full forty-five minutes after swallowing. The drugs were being tested for their effects on bone density loss, with the grand hope that they might somehow prevent breast cancer metastasis to the bone. "I decided against it," I shared, to which my senior colleague replied at top volume across the room that she decided to go for it because *she* was only in her fifties and "didn't want to die," because *she* "wanted to live to see her grandchildren." Then she described an aunt who died of breast cancer—"phht"—just like that. She cut her hand across the air the way Mike the tailor had done in telling his more hopeful story. "One day she got the diagnosis, and the next day she was gone!" I look toward another freshman in the room and roll my eyes. I clench my teeth and whisper, "Is that something we really need to hear?"

I imagine the senior and me coming to fisticuffs. Half-naked, we'd tear at each other's gowns, we'd pull at each other's hair and come up empty, we'd bite and scratch the way women in institutionalized settings do in prisons and insane asylums in the movies. We'd turn the waiting room into bedlam, and ourselves into figures out of *The Snake Pit*. I draw a blank at the point of picturing our punishment. Would they put us in the closet where they keep the goose's seasonal wear? Would they not *allow us* to be zapped for a day? Would they call our parents?

There is something about institutionalized settings, not merely the fact of lockers, that produces regressive dynamics between humans, but community, too, is maybe ill-fated the more it's ready-made. Ire might be expected if what people find they share is suffering, mortality, the mark of cancer, humiliation, discomfort, or despair. "What we're doing for one another here just by talking. This is medicine. Maybe even better medicine than the radiation," one senior tells two others in the far corner of the room.

"You dropped something, darlin'." He turns temporarily toward me.

"Oh! I knew this would happen one of these days! There were no lockers available today, so here I am dropping my bra on the floor for all to see! How embarrassing!"

"We're all friends here, darlin'. Ain't nothin' to be embarrassed about," and he turns back to his group to ask, "What do they call it? There's a name for what we're doin'."

"Psychotherapy," another answers, and I think, yes, sometimes what unfolds in here is the spontaneous emergence of support group chatter without a moderator, whether you want a support group or not.

What I want I think some days in radiation is music like I've never wanted music before. But not any kind. The kind that young composers write for French horn and strings, oboe and piano, and perform for small audiences awaiting inspiration and fiery light. I want nineteenth-century genre paintings depicting the sublime. I want a Unitarian naturalist's collection of seashells. What I get instead is the shocking view of another human being's misshapen, burnt, and blistered buttocks through the partly opened curtains of the locker room, and the feeling that I don't know why I'm being made privy to this view when I should be teaching. I don't know where the fuck I am, or, for that matter, who.

What we are in radiation's waiting rooms are people who have cancer. That's our identifying grate and grid and common ground. That's our secular blessing and daily bread, and it equalizes us like nothing I've ever known. Because we don't know anything about one another or what each one does outside of this: because of where we are, we know what other strangers cannot know about us without its being told—we know we all have cancer. Cancer is the turbulence that gets us talking lest we crash without the chance to say good-bye.

We want that closeness and we hate it too, and to deny it altogether, there's TV. A senior moves from her part of the room to mine. She sits down next to me, so I begin to talk until she explains she chose this place to get a better view of the TV. Some crazy days everyone inexplicably stops talking except to comment on the story on the waiting room's TV. Now we're a dysfunctional family who can't be together without the television's catatonic blare, we're heavy with the burden of an elephant in the room, or elephants in competition because the television is awfully big but silent even when it talks and our cancers are evident but invisible to the naked eye, just like radiation, and our bodies could be lumbering and thunderous as an elephant's, but we'd like to deny their power and disappear, to turn away from the death working within us, within everyone who's alive.

A teenager on the screen bears the label "practices abstinence," and I laugh, but the woman who has come beside me to get a better view stresses the importance of teenage sexlessness and how she took her daughter, and her husband had better take her son, to their church for discussions of this very thing. A newscaster has "lost his battle with cancer and will be greatly missed" (impossible to change the channel); the re-routing of interstate 195 has caused gridlock; the city's failure to respond to a snowstorm has caused mayhem. A cyclone that has hit Bangladesh draws a great deal of sympathetic sighs—the *lack* of resources over what we *have*—but isn't what we have in this First World waiting room our cancer?

It's possible that the degree of alienation we each feel is in direct proportion with the degree of our common ground, which is vast. Our cancer. There's a woman, a fellow patient, who reminds me of my Sicilian aunts and my Sicilian grandmother, whose large hands and voluminous bodies my small child body enjoyed getting lost in, who were tough and gentle and harried and sad, and who poured their worries into the wide-brimmed pots, cauldrons really, of the escarole soup they perpetually stirred. *Bosomy* women, unlike my small-breasted self, who were brassy and loving but who I could never know well enough because they thought the measure of their worth was in their sacrifice. At Thanksgiving time this woman who reminds me of my relatives makes over-the-top jokes about being "roasted" in the radiation room and the question of whether we'll smell her cooked flesh, and she waves good-bye to the entire group of us each day with a sweep of her large arm as she exits, as if from a stage or the deck of a ship leaving port before the days of airplanes. On her last day of treatment, she passes me in a separate room where I wait to see the doctor. She tells me she's heard that I'm a teacher and asks where and what I teach. When I tell her I work at the university, she asks if I have a Ph.D. and wants to know my last name. I think she's trying to place me, to consider if she might know me through people she knows at the school, but it's to give me this name that she's asked me, as if to know how to address me: "Dr. Cappello," she says, and I'm struck by the strange deference implied by her wanting to entitle me inside these rooms where our status is told by our clothes—by our gowns ye shall know we are not doctors but patients, by our gowns ye must know we never shall be doctors but always what we are. In the radiation waiting room, I'm a Dickinsonian nobody only conferred a somebody by my disease, just like her. Still, she insists, "It's been so nice to meet you, Dr. Cappello," "I wish the best for you, Dr. Cappello," and suddenly I feel myself assuming a sort of *face*, the bright face that I bring to a classroom, but it's very out of keeping with the gown and I feel silly. There's nothing like being authorized, and my cancer colleague's insistence that I am an author *of* something, an authority *on* something, though who knows what, even though we know my authority is meaningless here, makes me want to cry. My fellow patient's calling me "Doctor" feels as though she's agreeing to greet the delusional psych wardmate as the prince she knows he thinks he is, but I also feel her wanting to give me something real but out of reach, to dignify me even from inside the space of her own suffering. My cohort kisses me and leaves, her days of radiation are over. "I wish the best for you, Dr. Cappello." After she leaves, but only then, I begin to cry.

～

There's a moment in Roman Polanski's xenophobic thriller, *The Tenant*, in which the main character, Monsieur Trelkovsky, played by Polanski himself, performs a soliloquy that I've always loved.

Trelkovsky is a Pole living in Paris who becomes increasingly paranoid following his move into an apartment whose former occupant has thrown herself out of the window. The even eerier detail is that she didn't succeed in killing herself: Trelkovsky visits her in a hospital where he finds her wrapped in a body cast that makes her seem more like a mummy than a living being. Assuming she won't be returning to inhabit her apartment, the proprietors of the building, a sloop-shouldered figure and his plump wife, like a wobbly-faced couple out of *Rosemary's Baby*, have rented the apartment to Trelkovsky, complete with the hospitalized tenant's furnishings and clothes. As the film unfolds, it's hard to know if Trelkovsky's psychotic identification with the apartment's former inhabitant is a product of his own imaginative projection, or whether the people who form the social body of which he tries and fails to be *a part*—his fellow Parisians—are foisting that insane affiliation onto him, as if to say the Pole will never be a Frenchman, but if he wants so badly to be one, if he wants to fit in, he can only do so by becoming Mademoiselle Choule, the woman who formerly lived in his apartment and who was driven mad there. There is one tender moment in the film in which Trelkovsky is taken to a party by a woman played by Isabelle Adjani. Everything about her suggests a woman without hang-ups, and she has long hair to match her psychosocial demeanor—she's a person with whom one can let down one's hair. So, for a few hours in her presence and out of range of his menacing dwelling place, Trelkovsky begins to relax enough to release himself from his daily terror. He's nearly buoyantly feeling, for a moment, human, and he's also drunk, when he shares with her the tantalizingly lucid philosophical account of the split that haunts him. In his unforgettable monologue, which he makes while Adjani's character undresses him for bed, he asks:

> "At what precise moment does an individual stop being who he thinks he is? You know, I don't like complications. Cut off my arm. I say, 'Me and my arm.' You cut off my other arm. I say, 'Me and my two arms.' You . . . take out . . . take out my stomach, my kidneys, assuming that were possible. . . . And I say, 'Me and my intestines.' Follow me? And now, if you cut off my head . . . would I say, 'Me and my head' or 'Me and my body'? What right has my head to call itself me?"

It's possible that splitting is the keynote of a course of cancer treatment, but its epistemic ground is multiple and shifting, just as the rivenness occurs both *within* oneself and *between* oneself and others. Before my surgeries, I was aware of a new form of self-regard. I felt split at the level of knowledge, of mind, because it seemed to me that something was going to happen to my body that *I* was prepared for but of which *it* was unaware. Rather than feel "betrayed by my body," as the manuals tell us we are sure to feel when we receive a cancer diagnosis, I felt badly for my body. I perceived my body as innocently going along, doing its thing, unaware of what I knew was going to happen to it during surgery, unaware that *it* was going to be anaesthetized, cut into, rerouted, excised. I imagined my body as innocent of any knowledge of surgery's impending attack. Our bodies are ourselves, to nearly quote the famous feminist guidebook, but here I was anthropomorphizing my body as if to say the body on its own isn't quite a person; as if to say the body as organism was without consciousness, it was me and not-me, and in order to make it wholly me, I had to differently redouble it as human.

Chemotherapy was just as invasive, and one would think the idea of a split-off foreknowledge, a kind of head-as-experience and body-as-innocence routine, would have replayed itself here, but with chemotherapy I felt the configuration of part to whole self differently yet again. "All of me, why not take all of me"—the famous musical riff could have been chemotherapy's lyric. Both I and my body were chemotherapy's innocent recruits because chemotherapy, entering the bloodstream and auguring disaster to all rapidly producing cells in its midst, would leave no molecule untouched; in fact, it would leave me to construct a new body.

Radiation, supposedly "the easy part" (and didn't the technology put one a little in mind of those beauty parlor headpieces that whole generations of women enjoyed?) created yet another kind of seam. Now I experienced my breast alone as a part, a newly birthed appendage that, on the one hand, was becoming increasingly differentiated from its formerly symmetrical bedfellow—my other non-cancerous breast, no longer a twin but an odd fellow, the unscathed alongside the scathed—and on the other hand, was morphing into a hardened, brittle-feeling twig that, from the effects of radiation's burns, I felt, could, if I pushed it in a particular direction and with just so much force, actually *fall off.*

In radiation mode, I begin for the first time to feel scarily detached from people I consider my closest friends. I begin to experience split identifications: I have a profound daily allegiance to strangers in waiting rooms, while I perceive a gulf in social situations with people who do not hail from cancerland. Yoked to any regime long enough, one becomes subject to and subject of its sentences even if one resists thinking of oneself as a cancer victim, patient, or survivor. It's the crisis routine and its attendant uniform—the gown—that has put me and my cancer mates into a world apart, but neither is that world flush with connections: it's uncannily liminal. "At what precise moment does an individual stop being who she thinks she is?" After a month of daily trips to the hospital for radiation treatments, I begin to feel distant from those I know well and close to those about whom I know nothing.

I had no way of knowing that something as banal and anonymous seeming as my shoes would become the locus of my identity in radiation, at least where the radiographers were concerned. We know my reason for being here is the presence of a life threatening illness, and we know what they're doing to me has to be as deep as the reach of my aberrant cells' will to live. But we don't talk about that. Instead, we talk obsessively about my shoes. One of the radiation therapists and I determine early on an astonishing connection: we were born on the very same day in the very same year. I recite my mantra daily. Date of birth? October 22, 1960. My birthmate perhaps begins to feel not just a familiarity but a *famil-*

ial-ity therefore between us, or at least that's what I conclude by her questions about my personal life. Casting about, in search of further points of contact, adrift, she wants to determine what else we might have in common. "Do you have kids?" she asks me. "Yes," I reply, "other people's kids. Tons of them. I have all sorts of kids as a teacher." "Oh, but you don't have kids of your own?" She seems disappointed. "How about pets?" she asks me, only to learn that I'm a cat person and she's a dog person. Definitively. I swear at one point I hear her ask me if I have anything or anyone *at home*, and I swear I try to indicate the woman in the waiting room with whom I've arrived each day shares my home, but my lesbianism never enters into our language.

One day, as I assume my position on the table, she fastens onto my shoes: Keen-brand black winter wear, hiking-like walking shoes. She has lots of questions for me about these shoes, as does my peanut buttery-smelling therapist, Bob, until I find myself actually pushing the shoe of one foot off with my opposite foot (I'm on my back, and am not allowed to move my arms or hands), so they can better inspect the shoes, to read the shoes' details inside and out. The conclusion is a practical one, and one lit by desire: perhaps I would like to get myself a pair of shoes just like these, my therapist explains to me that this is what she's thinking. They're warm and comfortable and don't look bad and would be perfect for navigating icy pathways at 6:00 a.m. as she crosses the frozen tundra to the hospital.

For the shoes to enter our exchanges once or twice would not seem out of the ordinary. But the shoes, my Keens, begin to figure nearly every time we meet. Like the day on which I see Bob outside of the radiation room in a different part of the hospital. We greet each other knowingly and with smiles, after which a brief silence ensues which he immediately fills with a weird non sequitur: "My wife tried on a pair of Keens the other day." What can one reply? The range of things that one can say about any pair of shoes is probably wider than we give our imaginations credit for, but I thought we'd already covered a great deal of territory, having discussed whether Keens ran large or small; having determined the size and name of the model I was wearing (the Juno); having rated the different styles available to men or women; having noted how well they accommodated orthotics (my birthmate and I had pronation in common); having shared tidbits each of us knew about their Rhode Island inventor and Keen's telltale reinforced toe tip (the manufacturer had been a yachtsman who thought a person should protect his toes from stubbing, whether at sea or on land); and, of course, having also discussed their priceyness and the likelihood or lack thereof of finding these shoes on sale.

"I'm still not sure I should buy the shoes."

"My husband tells me, 'Will you just buy the shoes already'?"

"Have you seen her shoes? I'm thinking of getting a pair of these."

I don't always see the therapist who can only talk to me about my shoes, but as I'm readied for my treatment on the table, another therapist tells me she's to relay a message from her to me.

"She isn't here today," she says, "but there was something she wanted me to tell you."

"Something about the shoes?" I ask, and she says, "Oh, yeah, it had to do with shoes. She wanted me to tell you, she *got* the shoes."

I begin to think I'm being addressed in code. Shoes must be a stand-in for something else, and I haven't yet discerned it. Shoes is our secret agent language. It's what bonds us. Alternately, I become paranoid: I must be crazy and they know this but I don't know I'm crazy (one definition of crazy) and they've been instructed "only talk to her about shoes; otherwise she goes off the deep end." Or maybe they had a petty gambling ring going on the side, and they had bet each other that the shoes couldn't sustain daily mention. Maybe this was a fraternity prank: they *dared* each other to bring up the shoes each time they saw me. Maybe this is who I was because nothing about my upper body, begowned, marked me (though I did wear large black glasses). I was the patient who wore a particular kind of shoes. We were connected at the shoe.

One day my birthmate began to stroke my head. Just like that. There is something poignant, nearly helpless, about daily being made to assume the position, and for less than a split second, I thought she might be expressing a silent form of care. She didn't just touch my head. She ran her hand across it while I was lying on the table. My hair was just starting to come back in, and it looked like a thin, black pelt. After a moment, I realized she wanted to know what my hair felt like. She was touching me out of curiosity for newly sprouted down. She was *petting* me. The great film director, Eisenstein, notes that the inclusion of a furry creature in a scene will always incite sympathy. A cancer patient's head, like a pregnant woman's belly, is public property.

The shoes had a runic aspect that both distanced me from my radiologist and yoked me to her. They were a conveyor of something, but of what, I'm not sure. Sneezy, though, often said cryptic or indecipherable things to me. Like the day he told me, while positioning me in place, "You're not going to get a hippopotamus for Christmas *this* year." What kind of oracular pronouncement was this?

"You're making my brain hurt, Professor Cappello!" "My brain is fried, Prof. Capp!" So my students would say when exiting my class, and now Sneezy was doing it to me. My friend Russell calls me on my cell phone to ask what he can contribute to a dinner we're making together, but I'm preoccupied with the hippo pronouncement. "What do you think this could mean, Russell? Have you ever heard this saying?"

"Why, no," Russell, a self-pronounced sufferer of epistemophilia, shares my befuddlement. "It sounds like something out of Ionesco. What are they doing to you over there? Radiation is absurdist!"

"You're thinking 'rhinoceros,' but I definitely heard 'hippo.' What's the difference anyway?"

His MacBook ever at hand, Russell runs a quick search for me and recites over the phone the details of the legendary, "I Want a Hippopotamus for Christmas" song, a novelty piece sung by ten-year-old Gayla Peevey, a child star of the Oklahoma City area, in 1953. When the song hit the top of the charts that year, a local promoter presented Peevey with an actual hippopotamus for Christmas which she donated to the Oklahoma City Zoo. The song was over the top rinky-dink kitsch, enough to make a person go ballistically existential, but I later saw on YouTube that it was many a person's favorite seasonal melody. I wondered what it meant that this was what radiation therapy was teaching me. But I also remained stuck on Sneezy's deciding that I wasn't getting a hippo myself. Was this because I was getting radiation instead? It seemed a terribly mean thing to say, but I considered that his aggression might be the result of his parents having named him after one of the missing Seven Dwarfs. He must have suffered taunts as a child and felt infantilized long into adulthood. Russell, aware of my feeling slighted by the hippo quip, gave me a hippo figurine on Christmas day, as if to tell me my real friends knew what I needed, even if to my mind, the hippo will memorialize Sneezy and his lore.

I won't say arcana was beyond me, because I also tried to forge connections with the staff by way of a slantwise relation to their work like the time I brought in one of my bakelite View-Masters and a very specific set of discs. Few people knew that I collected the discs that were made in the earliest days of the viewing device. Not the 3-D cartoons—they didn't interest me in the least—but the magical dioramas that, for each slide, each shift in narrative action, some unnamed artist had actually built detailed miniaturized interiors filled with Claymation figures who lived out their intricately fabled lives inside an otherworldly space. Other kinds of unusual View-Master images formed part of my collection as well: alongside *Alice in Wonderland's* overlarge body crouched inside a tiny house, I enjoyed a tour of Frank Lloyd Wright's *Fallingwater*, shots of Capri and Victoria, British Columbia, as well as all manner of *Euphorbiaceae* for the botanically inclined. Among the gems in my collection, I counted *The Stereofloral Radiographic Images of Albert G. Richards* that I had, just after receiving my diagnosis, seen in Los Angeles at the museum of curiosa, David Wilson's one of a kind Museum of Jurassic Technology.

If every living being had, not a soul, but a diaphanous essence; if each creature were reducible to the shape of a breeze moving through the blue-green veil that was its self, Richards had exposed those shapes radiographically inside of flowers. I brought the View-Master and Richards' images with me to one of my Friday sessions, and told Bob he could keep it over the weekend if he wished, but the staff wasn't much into radiation art, and they dispatched the toy back to me after one quick flip through its pictures. Using radioactive rays to picture things and using them therapeutically was different in ways I didn't understand, but I don't think this explained the staff's indifference to my offering of Richards' curious work. I think the bottom line was that they had a job to do from which I shouldn't distract them even as I remained radiation's subject and its student: returning to Richards' blue-grey columbine and jonquil, to his lunaria and lady slipper, to his clematis, calla lily, and rose, I began to consider what lay hidden inside his radiographic depiction of floral innards. I realized that the high energy rays to which he exposed the delicate blooms must also have destroyed the flowers' molecular structure, that for the sake of his mystical pictures, he destroyed each flower at its core. I noted also that the radiograph perversely bleached each flower of its distinctly differentiating color. To a radiograph's eyes, everything in the entire world was uniformly blue.

Radiation is a point of view, an interpretive method; how could it be a *glue* between the person who applied it and the person who received it into her pores? One morning, as I begin to drool, Jean notices a perfectly articulated circular patch of brown-red sunburn on my back. We wonder whether I should mention it to the doctor or if they'd think I was loony to report a mark on my back when they were clearly radiating my front. There is something awe-full about it, but it isn't my paranoia: the rays indeed had *gone right through me*, baking me from the inside out. My radiologists were daily burning a cantaloupe-sized hole through my body, that went in one side and came out through the other.

Jean and I try to take walks each day following radiation even if it makes her late for work. If I find myself looking down rather than up, it must be because the treatment is wearing on me, it must be because of the snow. I remember entire walks not for the scenery or sky, nor for the sounds or scents inside the air, but for the underside of other people's shoes: here's a mandala, a lattice work, a waffle-iron pattern, or pizzelle. Here's a beveled outline, a web-work of weight and balance, of propulsion and release. A brand.

Flames leap up. Flames move sideways. My treatment by radiation coincides with the unstoppable, devastating fires produced by California's Santa Ana winds.

When I watch a needle go into my vein to draw blood, I'm aware of how quickly the blood rushes into the vial, how rapidly I could, via one small opening, be drained of my entire life force. Fire moves just as fast along a fuse. One can only hope that cancer doesn't move like fire. One can only hope the cancer can be starved of its sustaining conditions—smothered—while keeping its host alive.

To undergo radiation is to treat fire with fire.

My cat likes to sleep beneath lamps, but these days I worry about her getting scorched, of the top of her head becoming blemished or her fur irreparably charred. The pain emanating from the nerve in my surgical arm returns during radiation. There's nothing quite like this pain in my experience: it shoots from the underarm into the elbow as though a torturer has applied an electrical prod there. During this time I want to say my pain is "radial." Radiation has given me the perfect word and one that would never have occurred to me without it, because it feels as though spokes and spikes are involved, a hub and attendant petals: my pain opens like a sunflower.

Radiation might be relative to "ray" (its form) or to a radioactive element (radium). It's said of pregnant women—"You look radiant!"—leaving one to wonder when else it has been said of one, when last it was said, if ever it has been said or felt. Radiance. We speak of "radiating good will," as though the verb is most at home with missionary work. Giving or getting vibrations isn't quite the same. Radiation's rays are below red and above violet in the spectrum. And what of fire's? What of fire? Come on, baby, light it. I can't think of radiation without thinking of ray guns, of *Astroboy*, *Speed Racer*, of *Star Trek*, of *Lost in Space*. I suppose I'm currently radiant insofar as, if I turned off the lights, it's possible I'd glow in the dark.

Radiance doesn't require color if we consider that tuberculars were thought of this way: the paler the better, the nearer to death's pallor, the more redolent of the heartbeat's afterimage, the more proximate to ecstasy. Maybe radiance isn't all it was cracked up to be. Unless we're thinking glowworms and fireflies. The last time I saw one, a "lightning bug," I did a little reading about them and was disappointed: I think I wanted the lightning to exist unto itself, to have its own flickering integrity. I think I wanted to learn that it was timed like a messaging system between creatures of the earth and stars. I think I hoped to discover that lightning bugs were once sea creatures who continued to think the ink-black night was ocean, and so they lit their way to see in it. I think I wanted to forget that for every lightning bug there was a child with a jar. Instead, I learned that, of course, the flashing light was pressed into the service of mating, and as with most species observed by man, the male's lights were brighter than the female's.

During this period of my body being made to glow, I have the demoralizing experience of being drawn on. The last seven sessions of a radiation treatment to the breast are called "the boost," which entails a targeting of the tumor site and nearby tissue to which stray cancer cells might have migrated during surgery. The doctor draws the area on with a fat black magic marker—literally, he runs a black smudge across the middle of my nipple and into the field above it where the tumor lay. He makes a crude ellipsis. Not until I see this drawing in the locker room mirror, though, am I truly horrified. Now I feel defaced. The ugly saturated shape marks a space where the lurid and the lumpen meet. It's seedy, like something that might transpire between a man and a woman in a film by David Lynch.

The ink the doctor used was not indelible, so I was instructed not to wash the area until my meeting with the radiologists that would occur the following day. The lotion I was instructed to use, however, took the marking off, so I had to undergo the effacement yet again. This time the intern rather than the doctor tried to map the area with a red magic marker in place of black, when I noted that her drawing seemed differently positioned and differently shaped than the doctor's had. She admitted, consulting my chart, that she hadn't made the most exacting impression on my breast, and now she tried to erase the figure she had made by daubing it with alcohol (the last thing one should apply to radiated skin cells) and blowing on it as though she were trying to repair a botched manicure. Soon the doctor arrived to redraw the sad obloid, like a noose in which my breast temporarily hung, my flesh no longer a part of me because designated, tagged like a cattle's flank, but without the same proprietary intention, yet still somehow violated. My skin no longer serving as a barrier or protective envelope but as a flat surface available for another person's game of tic-tac-toe.

In Catholic grade school, the Sisters of the Immaculate Heart had taught us that the body was a temple that needed to be guarded against defilement by ourselves or others, the body as tabernacle of the soul. While I understood that the sisters were bent on our remaining chaste, I took seriously the premium they wanted us to place on protecting our own bodies and those of others from acts of violence. Nevertheless, I enjoyed claiming my body by drawing on it from time to time, as children do. They write primarily on their hands—the answers to a test, the page number of a homework assignment, the combination to a locker, their new best friend's telephone number; or they give a knuckle a pair of eyes in the form of dots, draw a smile on the inside of a thumb, thus making a part of themselves into a live puppet, a creature from another planet whose wrinkled mouth emits words in tones a pitch above their more familiar voice.

To this day, I write in the margins of my books, even the most expensive ones. I circle words and underline, turn down the corners of pages, and fill the page's gutters with marginalia which makes my books unshareable. It devalues them toward future use and overvalues them. It makes them mine.

Marking the body is something people do to one another as a way of controlling one another, as a way of subjugating one another. Marking the body is something people do to recognize and identify with one another, too, leaving me to wonder about the eventuality of color-coded bracelets in cancerland. A person with cancer or a cancer sympathizer is enjoined to mark herself as such, to announce her cancer by wearing a piece of colored jewelry, but to what end?

One day on which I felt like retreating from my fellows in radiation's waiting room, I rifled through reading material scattered atop a table in the center of the room. I found a catalog produced by a company that went by the name, Chemo Savvy, filled with images of women's heads draped in colorful scarves or crowned with hats for all seasons. The women's smiles ranged from tight-lipped, self-satisfied smirks (a sign of their savvyness) to teeth-baring, full-fledged grins (a sign of their glee). In each case, a woman peered from the corner of her eyes and tilted her heavily makeup face, defying the ravages of chemotherapy with her fashion sense. The owners of the company had thought of everything—including a special garment that featured a "unique Roo pocket" meant for the discreet stowage of one's surgical drain. The booklet's dystopic implications were unnerving: that one industry begets another; that enough of the country's population finds themselves on chemotherapy as to constitute a consumer group; that breast cancer, in particular, need be accompanied by fashion sense; that the savvy person would be she who most successfully hid the signs of her cancer; that "chemo" and "savvy" could appear alongside one another, weirdly shadowed by the pet name that Tonto applied to his "master," The Lone Ranger—"Kemosabie," or "faithful friend."

One page of the Chemo Savvy catalog featured an astonishing key. In an era of color-coded terror alerts, it appears that every cancer has a color, too, to which it corresponds. "Choose Your Color for Your Pin, Bracelet, Key Ring, Magnet or Hat," the catalog commands, and then provides an indexical guide:

Brain—Grey
Breast—Pink
Cervical—Teal/White
Childhood—Gold
Colon—Dark Blue
Esophageal—Periwinkle
General—Lavender
Head & Neck—Burgundy/Ivory
Kidney—Kelly Green
Leukemia—Orange
Liver—Emerald
Lung—Pearl (Bracelet is white)
Lymphoma—Lime
Melanoma—Black
Multiple Myeloma—Burgundy
Ovarian—Teal
Pancreatic—Purple
Prostate—Light Blue
Sarcoma/Bone—Yellow
Uterine—Peach

The semiotic challenge of this cancer alphabet was beyond me. I remembered a bestselling self-help book called *What Color Is Your Parachute?* and imagined a new, popularly individuating guide in its stead, *What Color Is Your Cancer?* Breast cancer isn't reducible to one type of cancer, but the grid gets around that by sticking strictly to the affected body part. Otherwise, they might need to invent *grades* of pink for estrogen receptor positive breast cancer, or the more aggressive Her2Neu positive type, or to differentiate between inflammatory breast cancer, infiltrating ductile carcinoma, or lobular carcinoma in situ. Then, too, should a person in remission bear the same color as the person whose cancer had metastasized? Or was the latter category covered by General?

The rationale for assigning colors was bafflingly illogical: colors seemed meaningfully attached to their cancer when the color matched the organ (e.g., Brain—Grey), and arbitrarily imposed when no connection between the two could be discerned, even if the color seemed carefully chosen and rife with intentionality (e.g., Kidney isn't merely labeled Green but more precisely, Kelly Green). Sometimes a cancer was represented by the part of the body it originated in, and other times its medical name served instead (not Blood but Leukemia). A child body with cancer is a body without organs and warrants a category all its own—Childhood—and a color significantly dear: Gold.

Of course, in order to recognize a colored bracelet for the type of malignancy it stood for, a person would have to become a student of the list of signs, an undertaking all out of proportion with our collective agreement to learn and then remember that red means stop and green means go in traffic. That Teal and Burgundy appear repeatedly is no doubt an effect of translating cancer into merchandise, since those two colors only ever seem to exist in clothing catalogs to give their bourgeois audience the impression that our dollars could purchase something uncommon and out of reach. (Here one might recall that during the feudal period of the eighteenth century, only the nobility enjoyed the right to bright colors while the bourgeoisie maintained a monopoly on black.) What color was Teal anyway? Would you know it if you saw it? Or would knowing it be the sign that you were chemo savvy? Perhaps the idea here was to wear one's cancer as a point of pride in the way one wore school colors on a knapsack or sewn inside an academic hood, more regally, a coat of arms.

To color-code cancer is a way *not to see it*, but worse than this for a person facing the possible waning of the light is the violence the catalog does to color. What my doctor did to my body with the stroke of his magic marker, Chemo Savvy literally does to color: color as a body we diminish by marking it. To color-code cancer is to *draw upon* color; to blunt its signifying power; to make it into a sign. It's to drain the world of light, to make the world colorless after teaching me as a child to know different hues by name, after teaching me to name my body's various parts. Had the point of such lessons been to take me here?

I begin to remember, as if by way of restoring the chink in a mosaic, the beaded skirt of a glass goblet, the fading fresco in an overly bright corner of a chapel in which a bird sips water from a fountain en route to paradise. I begin to recall a meeting beneath a tree ringed with mulberries in Sicily. The man with whom we were staying gently shook the tree with a long and slender pick used for gathering cherries. The woman who was hosting us pointed an umbrella toward a scorching sky, with one quick movement opened it, then turned the umbrella upside down to catch the tree's descending fruit. There's a saying in Italian, *capo di ombrello*, that loosely translates as, "My head is like an umbrella, opening and closing, I'm trying to gather my thoughts, but can't," that must have the inverted umbrella in mind. Purplish red berries pelted the inside of Irena's green umbrella—or was it plaid?—like grain to a silo. Who knew so many could be gathered so fast? And our exclamations tried to match her orange blouse, her blue-grey eyes, her husband's shock of bright, white hair. Digital cameras had just arrived on the market, and every corner we turned took our breath away with unexpected clusters of color, blunt dashes of light and brazen shades, but the camera was consistently out of battery power. We could take the photos with another friend's 35 millimeter camera for which she'd only provided black-and-white film. We could remember the colors of everything we saw, she said, and paint them in when we returned home. We never did. Our memories couldn't retain the particulars of each meeting's colors, and we never found the time to tint the photos anyway.

Of course, black-and-white photos have their own allure if you properly intend them the way a piece of chalk applied with enough pressure to a blackboard brings something forward. When I return to teaching following my stint in cancerland, I feel like Rip Van Winkle returning to a world forever changed and during which he slept: the blackboards in Freedom Hall have all been replaced with whiteboards, the chalk with magic markers. Blackboards turn a room into a grotto, a quiet in-dwelling of contemplation, but white boards feel like billboards on which lessons blink like ads. Chalk leaves white or yellow dust on my clothes and on my hands, and I like that: I like that it shows me getting dirty, that it casts ideas as *stuff* that needs to be handled, that every pedagogical encounter involves a form impressed with fingers as of unshaped clay. "Who shall clap out the erasers today?" Sister Celine would ask at the end of a school day, the black hand of the white clock stuttering toward three. And a ruddy boy with freckled hands, or two boys together, would perform the ritual while the rest of us ran home, tripping over chaos with lollipops, emerald or kelly green, in our mouths, unforgiving and a little sweaty in wool uniforms, blue black and just as green. The black erasers made no sound—they were the sound of one hand clapping white and yellow clouds into the air.

And I began to understand the somnolent nature of color unless it was accompanied by a sound: the sound of the oboe met by the copper-colored chandelier; the sound of the wind and the grey bench on which we sat, looking out; the sound of people bustling; and the color of the eyes of one that peered at you. Does the thing that sounds remain colorless, or is it lent the color of the place where it arrives? Maybe this was why musical instruments were nearly uniformly the same in color, rarely flashy, mostly dark and muted. I began to understand life as an accumulation of diminishing hues and collective vibrancies, sometimes barreling through consciousness and sometimes stilling it at a memory's saturation point of color, holding a body in place, asking it to step into an edge of color, especially on stairs, or inclines, to liken inclination to the shifting colors beneath your feet. I began to think of color as a seasoned alertness because snow was still surprisingly white with each repetition of it. Of color as a lens, or a mood to enter together and get lost inside, as I wish to do whenever you wear your orange shirt. Never pastels. *Nespole* brown or *nespole* yellow depending on the time of summer and the relative ripeness of that Italian fruit. Color as speed or substance, as sieve or filter, as something more or less let in or out like the intensity of my love for you as measured by the swiftness of my gait or the amble that we lend ourselves so as to walk together.

Jigsaw of color. When light is named for rousing drinks like coffee colored or palliatives like wine. I do not dream in color, but I have dreamt *of* color, always in the beyond, outside of me, and toward which I'm moving, which is to say toward which I'm dying. It's better when I have no idea what color the flower will be, but it costs a lot in plants, and then the garden can't be planned, which had been, I'd told myself, the point of it.

If properly urged, pink becomes red. Blue ebbs. Grey drowns. Red expands. If properly urged. Our organs were either colorless or fairly monochromatic unless exposed to air, at which point it's anybody's guess what color would emerge from the inside out. Charcoal blunts. Lavender lies. Green emits. Brown scrabbles. If properly urged or mixed.

I was beginning to take stock of the conventions available for writing light and finding them paltry. Inventing new forms could be a reason to live. I asked a thirteen-year-old in my care to make Shakespeare's line, "So quick bright things come to confusion" her own, and she gave me better than my contemporaries: "So swimmingly glowing things come to aquamarine." "So quick stone walruses break to complexions." "So strange purple blobs end in interruption." "So cold lighted lilies fall to the oceans." "So small strange dogs run to the market." I found another poet's line, Peter Gizzi's, turn inside a stanza—"All things partake of a signal green"—and wondered how it was possible that after touring a rock shop in Maine, yoked to our tasks like monks roaming in total silence inside the low-windowed roadside gallery of colors struck from all points of the globe as well as locally, Jean and I would choose the same glowing mineral as our favorite—a pale green stone veined with black and white, nearly lichen, most like algae. We were difference at a core but drawn to the same green point inside a field as likeness, as most like, as luring, as loveliest, and not quite round but shaped to fit inside a palm. Eyes are rarely green, but when they are, they communicate in a kind of code as though a slice of the eternal were deposited along the stalk that is an iris. Just as red hair—was it Thomas Merton who said this?—gives glory to God. And I began to consider that Gizzi might have us revisiting Andrew Marvell's metaphysical garden, "Annihilating all that's made / To a green thought in a green shade," more so than the "force that through the green fuse drives the flower" that drives Dylan Thomas' "green age," which was merely anatomical and much less true.

"The nectarine, and curious peach, / Into my hands themselves do reach" in the garden of Marvell's poem, and I feel flattered by the idea of an orchard dotted with the colors that are its tree's fruit, reaching; or how a sill is transformed by the ripening of its tomatoes or pears; or just by the fact of a lemon deposited there, drawing us, or drawing a day to its dawn. And I remember the ever available image of the grey cuckoo hidden inside leaves, of the scarlet tanager, just because its name was so replete. If I had seen in my day many a cardinal and blue jay in snow, I was just as startled by each approach of it. And I came to consider that pollen was never one color, though it usually came out yellow in artist's renderings even if it was more likely golden, like honey—see the furry crown of the pomegranate draping its tree—or even, inside lilies, black. That the fire engine need be red need not be questioned, but the antipodal relation of the color of smoke to the color of fire might.

During radiation, I dream I receive a bouquet made of nothing but rose stems, which I read as a sign of my fear that my cancer might spread like branches or use my body's bright pathways toward my doom. Long after radiation is over, I regard my skin in neon light and swear I see errant corpuscles sprouting there, as though my veins are a rash, as though in time I might break out of myself in living color. I remember the way my grandmother's arms bruised easily as a result of leukemia, unlovely colors. "Look what they did to me, Mary," and she showed me her arms streaked with long, red lines, but it wasn't the needles or the nurses' fault per se, it was the disease they never pronounced in my grandmother's presence for fear of informing her of the time she had left to live.

I know a writer whose cancer has been declared terminal. I send her music tucked inside a letter in which I write, "I understand very little." She replies, "I continue to write in my slow way, the poetry that has glued together parts of my life that make it whole." Can we all be kept alive long enough to fulfill our capacity for wonder? The poet tells me she will leave a wholeness in her work; but in equal measure, she leaves me with a baffling act. Because, for every writer, there is a lifetime's worth of journals, of notebooks, handwritten manuscripts, unsent letters, of works in progress, of manuscripts one did not wish to show. She will neither burn her work—consign it to flames—nor bury it: the two things we do to bodies when they die. She has decided to *bleach* the pages in the kitchen sink, in the bathtub, in any basin wide enough to take them in large batches, then throw them in the trash. But not before she soaks them long enough for the ink to rise, blue vanishing into white, from which it came, on which it wrote itself.

Strangers on a Train.
Notes from the Underground.
Repulsion.
It Happened One Night.

I was wondering if a book or film had already been written about the complexity of radiation's social dynamics that hadn't admitted its subject as such when the receptionist called to me, "Mrs. Cappello?" I was about to explain that I wasn't a Mrs. and that even if I were, I'd rather not be addressed that way, when I learned that it wasn't me she was calling but another Cappello. In fact, another Mary Cappello, who was much older than I and who sat facing away from the receptionist, staring sadly forward in a wheelchair.

"Are you Sicilian?" I ask Mr. Cappello, sitting next to the woman in the wheelchair.

"Yes."

"From a town near Palermo, called Belmonte Mezzagno?"

"Yes. Are you from Johnston?" he asks.

"No. From Philadelphia. But, hey, we *must* be related. Have you been there? I've been there. It's a very small town. We *must* be cousins. I've just met my cousin!" I yell to the receptionist. "What are the chances of that?!" But I can't get Mr. Cappello to speak in anything other than monosyllables, nor to crack a smile, which only tells me we must be kin: he's surly and gruff like my father.

Mrs. Cappello, Mary Cappello, is unable to take in the uncanny fact of our doubleness, the spark of a providential recognition, however meaningful or meaningless. She is possibly suffering from Alzheimer's disease or dementia. In the locker room, two nurses speak in front of Mary Cappello as though they assume she cannot understand them, as though she's been lobotomized. In the locker room, two nurses seem annoyed that they have to remove her sweaters so that she can be *put into* a gown, and as they push Mary toward the radiation room, they express impatience with her husband, asking him again, *please* to dress her in cardigans rather than pullovers each day. The Cappellos' situation is distressing, but I feel mostly aware of the fact that they cannot be, or, for whatever reason, will not be "my people."

The TV news reviews a new Rhode Island policy meant to crack down on undocumented immigrants. "They *want* things," a balding man in running shoes turns to me and says, "They're taking things from us." To which I reply, "You mean like our desire to clean toilets?" But he doesn't hear me and moves back to the TV before moving back to me. "Bilingual eduation! Have you ever heard of *that*?" "I wish I had," I say, "because I consider my not knowing the language of my forebears a considerable loss." If we're not in agreement, how can this conversation carry on? But it does, because the man sitting next to me covers over my challenge and seems to pretend his bigotry, momentarily, doesn't exist. "Where was your family from? Oh, they were Italian. Well, that's understandable. You wished you spoke their language. Of course. But, listen, what are the chances of my wife and me *both* getting cancer?" He adds the non sequitur.

And now it's as though a button has been pushed in my purgatory mate because he begins to spill numerous beans. He embarks upon a monolog. Our political differences don't matter so long as cancer is our ground, he seems to say. He doesn't stop for breath as he tells me everything about his case, and in between he learns my name so that he can occasionally insert me into the narrative. He addresses me as a fellow initiate, every now and then looking me full in the eye—"Mary, I know you know what I mean"—and I concur—"Oh, yes, Steve, *I* know what you mean"—because in a way I do. And the more he talks the more he reminds me of a professor I adored in graduate school who wanted me to sleep with him, but I refused, and whom I thanked instead for telling me all the dirt he knew about the woman I was in love with, because my knowing this brought her and me so much closer and gave our sex a fuller charge.

My waiting room companion's wife had just completed treatment for breast cancer when he was diagnosed with cancer of the stomach and the esophagus. He shows me the place, kitty-corner to his thyroid, where a prosthetic esophagus has been installed. He describes what eating feels like now—as though something is perpetually caught in his throat. The symptom of his cancer was raw and simple: one day, he just wasn't able to eat. He shares the horror of one day being told he had an 80 percent chance of survival, and the next day being told his chances were 50/50. Of how he walked through the halls of the hospital trying to smile, but how he felt he'd been punched in his already severely ailing stomach. "Oops, hold on," he holds up a finger, "I have to take this," and after hanging up his cell phone, he tells me that was his wife, to whom he applies the infantilizing euphemism, "She's a big girl," to describe her size. He tells me I won't believe what happened next, but he knows I'll understand, because the setting for this part of his story is his basement, which he's cleaned from top to bottom since getting his diagnosis, he's cleaned it—"*you* know what I mean"—in the way people facing mortality begin to put their things in order but also because, as a person facing his mortality, he wants to maybe use his rooms differently, to clear a room for a too long postponed woodworking project. "Of course I know what you mean, Steve," I say, and then he tells of how just following the establishment of the new/old space, he fell down the cellar stairs and broke both of his rotator cuffs. Steve punctuates each detail in his ever-mounting narrative by touching me on the wrist from time to time, but the nature of his hold on me doesn't originate in touching. It has to do with the thought of his manufactured esophagus and the flourish with which he hung up his coat, the spring in his step, his running shoes.

Certain things he can't afford to think about, he says, for example, the fact of his nephew being in Iraq. "He came back and wanted nothing more than to go back to Iraq again," he says of the boy soldier, and then offers up his idea of a "warrior class": every culture has one, and some people are just meant to be a part of it, so there's really nothing he can do about it. He's midstory when he's called out of his seat, but as he rises to leave, he shakes my hand, then he shakes both hands, and then he does something no other human being has ever in my life done to me. He bends my turned-around-black-baseball-capped head toward him, and kisses me directly on the top of my head. Sort of on the crown—he plants a kiss. Neither my forehead nor the front of my head, it was my corpus collosum that he kissed, as though I were an altar boy and he was a priest, as though I wore the zuccheto of a baby cardinal and he was giving me his benediction.

Often in radiation's waiting rooms I experience narratives like this: people tell me their stories with a trundling force, a blast of urgency, breathless accounts of trial without end out of which springs an unanticipated revelation, a conferral, or an annointing, whether I've asked for it or not.

There are too many lives to account for, to recount in cancer wards, but I tune in to another man's muttering even if the frequency is a monologic drone. I've met his wife in the locker room, a quiet woman. She barely looks up to say hello, while he draws a long thread across the silence strung with the pearls of everything that's on his mind.

"It's all in the book, but nobody wants to read it," he says. "Nobody wants to face it. I'm not a religious fanatic, I'm just saying what I know and it's there. All of the diseases, the wars, the violence."

"It's feeling apocalyptic to you?" I ask, at a moment when I can enter edgewise.

"It's there. My parents, my grandparents, aunts, uncles, cousins, sisters, nobody had cancer. Not like today. There's something different in the air we breathe. We don't know what we're drinking. What we're eating. Her sister died," his wife is still looking down, "her sister had it but didn't believe in questioning the doctor. She was old school. He was no good. I *told* her because I'd been to a seminar, I knew. I'm a bookworm. That's me. I like to read, can't help it. I *told* her that she needed to have it taken out, but this doctor who later was arrested for being an alcoholic, he gave her some pills and they made her sick and next thing you know it was in her back. It moved to the base of her spine. Oh, she was in a lot of pain." His wife nods. "Had to walk with a cane, so they moved her to a facility, what's it called?"

"Hospice care," I offer.

". . . for people who are terminally ill, and she didn't live long. She, here," he tilts to one side without looking at his wife, "she also doesn't ask questions, but I do. I tell the doctor, 'You're human,' I told one who talked down to us, 'You know what you are? You're NOTHING,' and he showed me the door. I say what I'm thinking, me, it comes right out," and he makes a gesture of something churning in his stomach and then coming out through his mouth.

"And I feel better, but we're all ending up in the same place. Six feet under. So don't act like you're something special. It's her body, you know," he points to his wife, "you know what I mean? We're all human. 'I don't care if you're a doctor,' I said, 'You're NOTHING,' and he showed me the door. My wife, she's Italian."

And at this point I realize she might not be comfortable in English, and this might explain her tendency to look away. "Where are you from?" I ask her in Italian.

"Napoli," she replies, and I tell her my grandfather was from nearby Naples, from Teano. "Ah," she smiles, "Teanese. You're Teanese."

"Yes, I guess so, Teanese," I repeat the word back to her, to myself, because this is the moment of my conferral, the moment of clarity I've been waiting for inside the long unwinding of her husband's poignant babble, because now I've learned a new word, a further origin.

"I like everybody," he goes on, as though nothing has emerged by way of punctuation, interruption. "I don't make any distinctions. You could be Jew, Muslim, speak Hebrew, I don't care. I have Korean friends, black friends, they all like me. I don't treat anybody differently. That's me. It's who I am. It's just the way I am. You can put your head in the sand like an ostrich, but that's no way to live."

My own head was beginning to feel as though it were perched on a very long neck, but I had no wish to bury it. My head was busy with listening, my neck perpetually craning, listening hard for the right word, the new sound I believed would come out in the song. Maybe we'd all be better off following the form of a Scottish friend of mine and her French colleague who has breast cancer. Her cancer is aggressive and advanced, my friend tells me, but every six weeks, they meet at noon, drink three bottles of champagne together, eat and talk until ten at night. And she's not a drinker, my friend reminds me, but she feels hypnotized—they enter this zone of hypnosis together, and the next day she can't remember a thing they've talked about, but it was important that they met.

~⌒⌒

"There's someone waiting for you," the receptionist points the way for me to make one more turn, one last pass around the radiation goose following my last of thirty-five treatments and more good-byes. "Who could be waiting?" I ask Jean as I gather my coat and brace for the wind tunnel that leads out to the parking lot. I saw the scarf of the woman from behind. She was undergoing chemotherapy and radiation simultaneously. I still didn't know her name, nor her type of cancer. I only experienced her as "the nicest person you'd ever want to meet." A beautiful woman with the delicate, pointed features of a girl in a painting by Degas. "I knew it was your last session," she said, "and I wanted to say good-bye to you and wish you well."

"All of this is very moving," my friend Jim says when I tell him on the phone of this farewell encounter. "I don't know what kind of cancer this woman has," I say, "I never found out. But she would have pockmarks on her face after treatments which made me think she must have to position her head face down, or press it against a grate."

"Yes, yes," Jim says, "but can I acknowledge that you're *finished* and I'd like to know what you're going to do to celebrate?"

"We're going to my favorite restaurant tonight with closest friends. Yes, we've got that planned."

"Alright, then!" Jim seems pleased. But I want to say that I might be finished with this phase of treatment, but I'm not yet finished with my story. Because I don't think I ever told him about the children we would see from time to time, and how heartbreaking it was, and how I'd talk past my own grief in watching them by cursing, "Children shouldn't have to go through this shit!" On Thanksgiving day, for instance, the girl attached to an IV, tucked all the way under a homemade blanket atop the pocket of the wheelchair that held her tiny body. Or the boy who was just a dot of orange in an enormous sea of green sheets. I wonder about the effects of radiation on their still-developing bodies, their tender frames.

Children should have the last word in cancer's narratives, but what I notice about the child I observe most in radiation is that she refuses to speak. Only one of us remains silent in radiation's hallways, busy with chatter, desperate with banter, neck-deep with technology's gloating. She walks as slowly as it takes a bud to open, tentative; she is always holding her mother's hand. "So, are you going to tell me your name today?" Silence. "So, still no talking today then?" Silence. "Not even an 'hello?'" The receptionists and therapists repeatedly try.

The child is the only person who understands the risks involved in speaking. That trust is never freely given or received. Only the child is courageous in this way: unwilling to give the other what she knows he wants to hear. Unwilling to speak a familiar language in this foreign land.

I try to glean her high forehead, her head not entirely without hair, her wisps.

My last day of radiation is strangely emotional. I start to feel tears well up around saying good-bye because release is sweet, but it reminds me of all that I've been carrying; release is sweet, but I'm discouraged and afraid of what I might find on its other side. My birthmate's parting words are inconclusive: "I got the shoes," she says, "for half their original price. But I couldn't find them in black, so I got the reddish ones." She seems unsure.

"The red ones are great. I know which ones you mean. I love that color. They'll be more distinctive in maroon, and just as versatile," I say. "So why aren't you wearing them?"

And she replies, sighing, "Would you believe they're held up in Oklahoma? I ordered the shoes, but they're stuck somewhere in Oklahoma." *Oklahoma, where the wind comes sweepin' down the plain, And the wavin' wheat can sure smell sweet, When the wind comes right behind the rain.* This is all I know of Oklahoma, and that its city zoo's hippo was one time tied to a girl and her song. Of hippos, all I know is a love of mud and waddle, their overlarge nostrils, and ferocity. "You've got to be kidding me," I say, "stuck in Oklahoma? How strange!" I don't reveal what could truly be meant by this, what she's really trying to say, something they've all been trying to tell me, if only we could connect and our meanings could come clear. I only know it's a message about my fate, my fate, and that of a hippopotamus.

Called Back:

the voyage out

I write to give a form to all that lingers. This strangely prescient gift: to recollect the person who had opened, dug out, and closed me on a summer afternoon, who had entered at an apex, fleshed my flesh, and fought misgivings at a core.

Moving out from cancer treatment doesn't happen like a cut-and-dried stepping from a sea onto a shore. Remnants linger like foggy thinking and blurry sight. It can take days, if you have the opportunity, to de-medicalize your house, and some corners, in spite of sweeping, will retain a whiff of reliquary. In one part of a room, I stow an oblong box designed for fancy tea bags that now contains my once-sprung hair. My mother had sent me special pasta in the box, and I decided it was just the kind of sturdy keeper—black and deep with corners reinforced—to hold my bits of black excelsior. Someday the box could find the piece of china or fragile figurine that it was meant for, because the hair really seemed like stuffing, or a buffer awaiting a weight it could secure.

Will life allow you now the time it takes for senses' slow return?

204 • MARY CAPPELLO

I don't realize that it's raining until I see it in the headlights.

I decide to eat the mint leaf whole that graces gourmet ice cream.

On the last day of radiation, I move myself to resume some simple tasks, but feel ambivalent about watering my plants. I have so many that it usually takes an hour to move from sink to plants and back again, and I feel tired. At some weighing station along life's highway, no doubt in adolescence, I paused to read an article, one sentence of which I still retain: *not* watering one's plants, it had said, was a sure sign of depression, so even when I feel depressed, I force myself to water.

Rounding the corner past the jade plants and neglected bonsai spruce, wondering how to reshape the hibiscus and if the night blooming cereus will learn again to thrive, I contemplate resumption. It's a routine watering, but I'm met by a surprise: two long stalks thick with tight, white budlets emerge from the leaves of a plant I had considered chucking. The person I had purchased it from had told me it was an orchid relative: its leaves were purplish brown, mildly velveteen, and salmon-veined; its limbs were succulent and strangely gnarled, but it never seemed to grow. Certainly, *never* had it flowered.

"It's happening again," I think, "my life a story told in nature. The world abundant with signs all meant *for me*," because who wouldn't read the sudden blossoming at radiation's close as somehow meaningful?

"Did your plant *talk* to you?" ten-year-old Natasha asks me later that night: she has my ticket, she reads me like a book.

What calls you and to what will you respond? For how long will you refuse to be seduced or pretend you weren't seductive? *"Call* me when you get a chance." "Did you get my *call*?" What does it take for any of us to *enter into*? Recall my saying so but don't call me back like damaged goods gone out with flaws and now inoperative. *Call back.* It's what we want from fellow humans, it's the phrase we use to say "You got the job!" or that we *want* you. And so the feeling has got to be obverse when you're perversely called back inside the world of mammograms because the picture was too telling, or because it wasn't clear.

Returning to work, I feel like a hovercraft wondering where to touch down and when. Do I read student papers and prepare for an upcoming class? Do I plan like a fiend for a meeting I'm in charge of? Do I make travel arrangements for a reading I've agreed to give on some far-out spit in the middle of a bay? Or do I finish out the writing of this book—finish out, for lack of a better phrase—"because it's just that close. And when I bring it to its conclusion," I tell a friend, "I'll be released again into the work my cancer treatment took me away from." Away and back, not ever fully either, but differently turned toward: called back.

Instead of touching down, I walk. Instead of turning back too soon, I walk and walk this day and think of cats—who don't come when you call them, like humans or like dogs, which isn't to say a cat won't respond to a signal it associates with a reward, a pleasure its been trained to want. A cat like a child dithers rather than responds when it is called. A cat refuses. A cat remains. A cat has better things to do than heed your calling.

Can I refuse to come the next time cancer calls me? *"I heard, as if I had no Ear / Until a Vital Word / Came all the way from Life to me / and then I knew I heard."* Emily Dickinson's stanza seems as though it has a calling in mind, and a religious or spiritual one at that, but since we know she refused the evangelism of her day, it's impossible to rest assured her *vital word* was the word of God, just as, on the face of it, you'd want to say my *vital word* was "cancer," but I'd resist that.

Are last words the same as vital words? "Called back" were Emily Dickinson's last words inside a letter to her cousins, an entire letter in two words, "Called Back," and later carved, the words appeared on her tombstone at the behest of her niece. *Called Back* was the title of a novel that had haunted her, and the perfect final signature because it did not cancel yearning.

Following my first post-treatment mammogram, I can barely see to read the words that Dr. C. holds up before me. She's presenting me with something like a platter upon which might sit a splendid fish that I'm to notice and respond to, but I can't see to focus. Neither a specimen nor a slide, nor an image of my insides, it's just a sheet of paper lined with words: "Normal" and "No sign of cancer in right breast." At home, the news is confirmed a second time with a letter that the postman slips through a slot—the kind a writer is used to getting, of acceptance or rejection, of the grant awarded or denied—with the major difference that this was nothing I'd applied for but something for which my body had signed up: "We are pleased to inform you that the your [sic] recent mammogram done on 2/20/2008 shows no evidence of cancer."

"Done on" seems nearly ungrammatical, but I'm forgiving. I want to know now how I will monitor myself for signs of a recurrence. I know, because my surgeon teaches me, that a recurrence of an original cancer is worse than a new cancer—she uses the phrase "more ominous"—because it means the disease resisted all that medicine had to offer. "You live your life," she says, pushing me forward with her eyes, "and leave the monitoring to me."

"You mean, I can go now?" I almost want to ask, like a truant who has been kept behind to write some words a thousand times upon a board. "It's ok for me to go?" *I will no longer be late for school, I will learn to be on time, I will come when I am called.*

"You live your life," she says. Such sweet allowance, such profligate permission. I want to hug my surgeon, but I resist. I know she knows it's not so simple—this demand to live my life and not watch out for cancer and not attend its silent call. But I hold fast to a schoolyard image: of a door flung open by a grade school nun who held me for a time and taught me things, in whose care I'd been, who knew nothing of my art or my imaginings, who helped me once and then let loose the door.

Past the clapping of erasers, past a clock recounting sums, past the letters of a story falling like a thrum, past the fences hung like twine, past a honeysuckle vine, past the crossing guards—their sashes—past their funny names, "the Safeties," with what unguardedness, with what assurance, with what undying breathlessness, I run.

AUTHOR'S NOTE

The letter-poem of Emily Dickinson cited herein is an excerpt of Letter #199 in Ellen Louise Hart and Martha Nell Smith's, *Open Me Carefully: Emily Dickinson's Intimate Letters to Susan Huntington Dickinson*, Paris Press, 1998, 217–18. All citations from Marcel Proust's *Swann's Way* refer to Lydia Davis' new translation (Penguin Viking, 2003). The phrase "ritual in transfigured time" that appears in Chapter Four has Maya Deren's experimental film of the same title in mind. The film (made in 1946) was an inspiration in the writing of this book. Grateful acknowledgment is made to *The Georgia Review*, and to *The Seattle Review* where versions of Chapter One and of the Coda appear.